Whatever Happened to Delight?

Whatever Happened to Delight?

Preaching the Gospel in Poetry and Parables

J. Barrie Shepherd

Westminster John Knox Press
LOUISVILLE • LONDON

Scripture quotations marked NRSV are from the New Revised Standard Version of the Bible, copyright © 1989 by the Division of Christian Education of the National Council of the Churches of Christ in the U.S.A., and are used by permission.

Scripture quotations marked RSV are from the Revised Standard Version of the Bible, copyright © 1946, 1952, 1971, and 1973 by the Division of Christian Education of the National Council of the Churches of Christ in the U.S.A., and are used by permission.

See acknowledgments, p. 145–146, for additional permission information.

Book design by Sharon Adams
Cover design by Night & Day Design

First edition
Published by Westminster John Knox Press
Louisville, Kentucky

This book is printed on acid-free paper that meets the American National Standards Institute Z39.48 standard. ∞

PRINTED IN THE UNITED STATES OF AMERICA

06 07 08 09 10 11 12 13 14 15 — 10 9 8 7 6 5 4 3 2 1

Library of Congress Cataloging-in-Publication Data

Shepherd, J. Barrie
    Whatever happened to delight? : preaching the Gospel in poetry and parables / J. Barrie Shepherd.— 1st ed.
        p.   cm.
    Includes bibliographical references (p.   ).
    Contents: A dearth of delight — An imagining God — Steps toward delight — Looking for the Resurrection — Delight in action.
    ISBN-13: 978-0-664-22781-4 (alk. paper)
    ISBN-10: 0-664-22781-3 (alk. paper)
    1. Preaching. 2. Sermons, American. 3. Presbyterian Church—Sermons. I. Title.
    BV4211.3.S535 2006
251—dc22

                                                    2005058465

I dedicate this book to my fellow students

at Yale University Divinity School

during the years 1960-1965,

with gratitude to God

for the many and varied

worldwide ministries we have served.

"For all the saints . . ."

Words, Lord,
  words upon words, upon words,
    miles of words,
      millions of words,
        mountains of words:
  words on paper,
    words on computer screens,
    words over telephones,
      words into microphones,
  words.

So we gather here to cherish words,
    to salvage words,
  to search among the trash heaps of this world
    for the right words,
      the few words,
        the precious words,
    the lively,
      singing,
        dancing,
          mending,
            moving words
  that witness to the gift,
    the grace,
      the glory.

We gather in the name of the Word,
  that Word of Life who invites us,
    calls us,
      claims us
        for this ordinary-sacred feast
      of wisdom,
        of hope,
        and of delight.

Let your Word now live
  and move
    and dwell among us.

Amen.[1]

Contents

INTRODUCTION

꧁꧂

How well I recall standing at the mailbox on an early spring afternoon in 2001 and opening, with some curiosity, an envelope from my alma mater, Yale University Divinity School. Unlike the address-labeled fundraising appeals that appeared there all too regularly, my name and address were actually typed onto this communication, and it felt lighter, not heavy enough to hold the usual enclosed return envelope. My curiosity turned to astonishment when I tore open the envelope and read the letter inside informing me that the faculty of the divinity school had voted to invite me to deliver the Lyman Beecher Lectures at Yale in October of 2002.

After the initial shock, I remember feeling a sense of excitement and even anticipation at the challenge this offered, and I fired off a letter of acceptance without much hesitation. After all, it would be great fun to return to Yale after almost forty years, and I had eighteen months, more or less, in which to think of something to say. Over the next few weeks, however, a more terrifying reality began to settle in.

Somewhere I found a listing of previous lecturers, names and dates since the inception of the series by

Henry Ward Beecher, Lyman Beecher's celebrated preacher son, in 1871. On that list I read such historic names as P. T. Forsyth, D. T. Niles, Henry Sloane Coffin, Harry Emerson Fosdick (who preceded me in the pulpit of the First Presbyterian Church in the City of New York), George Buttrick, Reinhold Niebuhr, that eloquent Scot James S. Stewart (recently named as the finest preacher of the twentieth century), under whom I had studied in Edinburgh, and W. H. Auden (whose poetry breathes its spirit through my own attempts at verse). And then there were the giants of my own era, several of whom I was fortunate enough to count, not only as role models, but also as friends: names like William Sloane Coffin, Frederick Buechner, David H. C. Read, Gardner Taylor, Phyllis Trible, James Forbes, Barbara Lundblad, Walter Brueggemann, Barbara Brown Taylor, and Peter Gomes.

Anticipation began to be replaced by intimidation. What were they thinking of to invite me, a common or garden-variety parish minister, to follow in that illustrious line of theologians, homiletics professors, literary luminaries, and the like? At the same time those long, luxurious eighteen months dwindled rapidly down to twelve and then six months, and the terrifying question remained: what was I to say? As was so often the case, my wife Mhairi broke the logjam. In her down-to-earth, common-sense way, she simply said, "Well, they must have had some reason for inviting you. You're not even a regular donor to the Alumni Fund, certainly not a potential "heavy hitter." Think about why they might have chosen you."

I began to look back over some thirty-seven years of preaching: a ministry carried out in Chicago's inner city, with the Chicago City Missionary Society; on college and university campuses, at the University of Connecticut and Connecticut College; in a small midwestern town setting, in Wooster, Ohio; in the gracious eastern suburban setting of Swarthmore, Pennsylvania; and in the vast metropolitan melting pot of New York City; a ministry that was always, at least in part, directed to college and university students and faculty; a ministry that had its roots sunk early and deep in the preaching traditions of my Scottish homeland, where the Sabbath preachments were major high points of the week, and our parish minister, former coal miner John A. Taylor, was a pulpit prophet with a shock of white hair, jet black eyebrows, and a voice that folk well believed might waken the dead someday. The story was that his hair had turned pure white in one agonizing weekend on the Anzio beachhead when he buried over one hundred of the young lads he had guided through training and preparations in North Africa during World War II.

What had I learned during these often turbulent years—for my ministry had spanned and been actively involved in both the civil rights movement and the protests against the Vietnam War, as well as the more recent movement to change attitudes toward homosexual persons within the church? Was there any vital message in all of this that I wanted to communicate to the next generation of preachers? Given "twenty minutes to save the world," as one of the previous Beecher lecturers had described the preaching task, what might I pass along about how to go about it?

My thoughts gradually began to focus themselves around what I call "The Art of Preaching," an approach to the presentation of the gospel that sees it primarily as an art form, as a craft, an act of genuine creation that participates, in some way, in that original creative act when, by means of the Word, the entire universe came into being:

And God said . . . And there was . . .

Over the years, in other words, I have come to see my calling in the pulpit to have at least as much in common with that of the poet, the painter, the composer, as with that of the news reader, the educator, or the philosophical debater.

My task, Sunday by Sunday, has come, through a long and often strenuous process, to be that of crafting a sermon, like the sculptor chipping away all unnecessary verbiage; like the playwright, struggling for forms of expression that convey far more than any mere collection of consonants and vowels; like the composer, striving to use assonance and dissonance, repetition and silence—perhaps especially silence—not merely to charm the ear, but to create mood, ambience and atmosphere, to evoke mystery, awe, and wonder.

Rather than seeking to frame a persuasive argument, to marshal fact and probability into something that might eventually convince the mind, I sought more and more to create a work of genuine art, something that reached for

the truth, yes, but reached for it via that other immortal
virtue, that of beauty, so that, as John Keats perhaps
would have it, beauty and truth combined evoke a wisdom that can truly reach deep into the heart of things, of
all things, T. S. Eliot's

still point of the turning world . . .

and discover there the essence of pure grace.

All of this led me to the central focus of my Beecher
Lectures, and what is, to me, the largely missing element
of delight in today's preaching—delight as a function
both of the sermons that are preached and of the response
of those who listen to those sermons. One of the problems—the occupational hazards one might call them—of
the regular Sunday preacher is that she or he hardly ever
gets to hear how other preachers do it. We are all "on" at
the same time, more or less, and so rarely have the opportunity to listen to what in other professions might be
called "the competition." However, during the latter
years of my ministry, with larger church staffs, capable
associates eager for opportunities to preach, and more
generous vacation and sabbatical provisions, I was able to
do some visiting, sneaking into back pews, and sampling
what was offered by my colleagues.

There were many—too many—occasions of sheer
boredom, to be sure. But there were also occasions, and
not a few, when my interest was captured and I learned
something new or relearned something long since forgotten. But the moments of delight, those times when I was
swept out of myself, and my own self-concern or even

self-improvement, and confronted with the sheer grandeur of God, the utter miracle of incarnation, the overwhelming power of the Holy Spirit, I could count on the fingers of one hand. It was this lack, this sheer absence of delight, and the little that I have learned about ways to address that absence, that I decided to approach during my five days at Yale in the fall of 2002. The book that follows is the result of that approach.

A final annotation concerning method. The following chapters have, of necessity, been modified and adapted from the actual text of the lectures delivered at Yale University Divinity School in October 2002. As one example, many of the introductory remarks, and specific references to personalities and events at the divinity school would be inappropriate for a wider audience. Again, the forms and manners of speech employed in a lecture setting often do not "translate" well into written form. At the suggestion of my editor, I have divided the subject matter of my third lecture in two, choosing to devote one entire chapter, chapter 3, to issues of method and approach, before attempting to pull everything together in chapter 4.

Also, as a part of Convocation 2002, I was the university preacher at Yale's Battell Chapel on the preceding Sunday morning, and that sermon, "Nothing Matters," along with two other sermons, is included in an additional chapter, chapter 5, as illustrations of the method proposed in those lectures and this book. Naturally, since these sermons were written for specific occasions and congregations, there will be no one-on-one correspondence between them and the contents of the preceding chapters. However, it seemed to me to be helpful to present them as one individual's attempts at recovering at least a few of the long-neglected delights of preaching and hearing that quintessentially good news that we have come to call "the gospel."

A closing word of appreciation is in order to Dean Harry Attridge, former Dean Harry Baker Adams, and the faculty of the Yale University Divinity School for their gracious invitation to me to present the Lyman Beecher Lectures for 2002; and to my wife, Mhairi, for her patience and encouragement throughout long and demanding months of preparation and the five exciting and exhausting days of their delivery. Looking back one more time on those preparatory months of mounting terror, I am beginning at last to appreciate the role of fear in the creative process, and the biblical insistence upon trembling before the presence of the living Word.

Chapter 1

A DEARTH OF DELIGHT

❊❊❊❊

Eye hath not seen, nor ear heard,
Nor have entered into the heart of man,
the things which God hath prepared for them that love
    him.
But God hath revealed them unto us by his Spirit.
For the Spirit searcheth all things, yea, the deep things of
    God.

1 Cor. 2:9 KJV

These familiar words of promise and hope have traditionally been regarded as a vision of the future, as describing, or rather pointing toward, that bright prospect that
awaits the true believer, the faithful pilgrim, stored up at
the end of time. However their context gives little justification for such an exclusively eschatological setting, and
it seems to me in fact that Paul is actually speaking of the
here and now, not of a future, but of a present and active
reality in the Christian life.

Eye has not seen, nor ear heard,
Nor have entered into the human heart
the things that God has prepared for those who love God.

It's almost like a treasure hunt, like one of those children's party games in which someone has hidden all kinds of wonderful surprises along with a series of clues as to where they might be discovered, and the participants progress from clue to clue, from one surprise to the next, moving now this way and now that, getting warmer, colder, warmer again, with a mounting sense of anticipation and sheer delight.

What a magnificent description of the Christian life! No long and dreary dragging down the path of duty and obligation. No grim enduring marathon of prayer and fasting, sacrifice of this and denial of that, with guilt as constant traveling companion. A treasure hunt, a journey rich with anticipation and potential, blessed every now and then with moments of vision, satisfaction, and joy, and continually guided by the Spirit who searches all things, the deep and fertile things of God, and reveals to us there the presence, the glory, and the grace of the Divine.

Now granted there is more to the life of faith than this, granted there are other equally valid and more somber images that will also guide our pilgrimage. But why are these others almost exclusively the ones we hear of? Why is this tantalizing and inviting image of Paul's generally ignored, or if not, then shoved off into the far distant future? Why are we—and we Calvinists have long been eminent in this area—so negligent at pursuing what our own Reformed tradition has long assured us is our *raison d'etre*, our chief end in life, and also in death: to glorify God and enjoy God forever?

In the High Kirk in Bathgate, Scotland, the church I

grew up in, a rectangular dome of glass hovers above the center of the nave. And around that radiant source of light, in elegant old gothic lettering, one can read the words, "Worship the Lord in the Beauty of Holiness." Yet as I sat in the balcony during my early teen Sunday school years, right under that dome and those richly lettered words, dutifully memorizing the answers in the Shorter Catechism, nothing was ever said, as far as I can recall, about actually enjoying God today, let alone forever, or how I might even begin to recognize the *beauty* of holiness when I saw it.

Why is it that so many sermons nowadays have so little genuine joy in them? Why do so many display such an absence of true beauty? Why do they seem to come across, less like a treasure hunt, more like an instruction manual, the bylaws of your condominium, or those assembly directions in four languages for whatever you just bought at the Do-It-Yourself store?

I am speaking of a dearth of delight. When the great Augustine in book 4 of *De doctrina,* the earliest homiletical text of the church, set out to define the goals of preaching, they were essentially threefold: docere, flectere, delectare— Latin for to teach; to turn, change or even convert; and to delight. I composed a poem around this triple-decker definition some years ago. It is called "State of the Art."

State of the Art
Docere, delectare, flectere,
to teach, delight, persuade . . .
the threefold task
of each and every preacher—

or so said Hippo's episcopos,
the magisterial Augustine.
Today we have our teachers,
making points to prove the ways of God
are not all that unreasonable after all.
The movers are still with us too,
battering Bibles, pulpits,
and their congregations' souls
with brutal bleak denunciations
of the wandering ways of humankind.
But where are those who can delight,
can wield the wide, wild, rainbow palette
of creation to portray those bright scenarios
may yet evoke a reborn glimpse of glory,
wonder, tears too, a sudden holy laughter,
yes and even—now and then—
some sheer astonishment?

It is my contention that in constructing Augustine's three-storied house of preaching, we relegate that third item, "delight," to the category of trim, of decor, rather than of foundation. Imagination becomes at best an optional extra, an upgrade, to be added if you really believe you can afford it—acceptable for those who are "into" that sort of artsy-craftsy, poetsy-literary, theology-lite kind of thing, but hardly appropriate for the serious preacher, or should I say the serious homiletician? The realm of the imagination, after all, is that of fantasy and fairy tale, is it not? Kids' stuff, in other words, not on the same level as solid theology or basic doctrine. "It's all in your imagination," we say, meaning it's not anything that has to be taken seriously.

Despite the somewhat amazing fact that ministers in

my own denomination, the Presbyterians, pledge in their ordination vows to serve God's people "with energy, intelligence, imagination and love," I never yet saw a committee on calls and credentials reject a candidate because of a critical lack of imagination. Indeed, energy alone seems almost too much to ask of some candidates. And when one turns to the governing bodies of the church—at least the Presbyterians—the situation seems much the same. In my ongoing pursuit of the ecclesiastical imagination, I checked out the fiction section of the Cokesbury bookstore during a recent Presbyterian General Assembly. In all that vast display, designed surely to appeal to what today's clergy are interested in—or feel they ought to be interested in—there were only two books of genuine fiction on offer.

A dearth of delight then; a homiletical landscape in which preachers believe their calling to be to instruct, to inform, to convict, to convert, but never—or in Gilbert and Sullivan's timeless phrase, "Well, hardly ever"—to amuse or even, perish the thought, to entertain. The one compliment you never want to hear in the narthex—and this belongs among the few firm homiletical persuasions I took away from my years of seminary training—is, "I enjoyed your sermon, Reverend." All kinds of other comments are acceptable:

> I appreciated your sermon.
> I learned from your sermon.
> I was helped by your sermon.

Or, from the parishioner during the Lenten sermon series on pain, "I never knew what suffering was, Father, until I heard you preach." But "I enjoyed your sermon" is most definitely out. Sermons—don't you see?—are not supposed to be enjoyable. Sermons are—in that "millstone-around-the-neck" phrase—supposed to be good for you. And any thought that a person might leave a church feeling amused, intrigued, enchanted even, let alone delighted, is out of the question.

> *Memento, homo, quia pulvis es,*
>   *et in pulverem reverteris.*

> Remember, O mortal, that you are dust,
>   and to dust you will return.

Yes, we are pretty good at recalling folk to their mortality, reminding men and women that they are dust. But what about that other ingredient from that creation story in Genesis chapter two? When do we get to also remind them about that breath of God that puffed a couple of vibrant lungfuls of divine life and breath—and, yes, inspiration too—deep into that selfsame heap of dust?

Some would trace the roots of this problem back as far as the sixteenth century, when both Reformation and Renaissance elevated the role of reason and, almost as a necessary consequence, deemphasized and devalued any role for the mysteries of the faith that had been so much a part of the medieval church. The preacher's job, according to Luther, was to seek out the *unum, simplicam, solidem et constantem sensum*, the "one, simple, solid and constant meaning" of the text. This was, of course, a necessary correction to the weird and wonderful (and often theologically irresponsible) flights of allegorical interpretation that typified much of the preaching of those times. But, as one quickly learns in skiing or in steering a sailboat, corrections can all too speedily become overcorrections, and the clear—but oh, so dry!—rationality of the preaching during the centuries that followed tended to leave no room at all for ambiguity or complexity of any kind, let alone mystery. Thus, as Rubem Alves, in his Edward Cadbury Lectures observes, "once all the gaps are filled by knowledge, we discover that the Word has lost the power to resurrect the dead."[1]

Some years ago I taught a senior-level course "Imagination in the Pulpit" at a Lutheran seminary and was both amazed and alarmed to discover that every student sermon handed in over the first few weeks was nothing more than an exercise, an often elaborate exercise, in balancing law and gospel. No matter where they began, that's where, by page three at the very latest, they ended up. I faced the students with this, informing them that, whatever they may have been taught at their Lutheran granny's knee, the enormous richness and vitality of the Christian gospel could not be permanently confined between these two otherwise highly commendable doctrines. And that, furthermore, I would not accept another sermon based on those two concepts alone. And, lo and behold, there were complaints from the theology faculty about what heresy this Presbyterian mole was forcing upon their best students.

The English scholar and monk H. A. Williams, in his book *True Resurrection*, traces a similar process in all religions whereby "the direct awareness of mystery" is gradually solidified over time "into creeds, orthodoxies and conventional ascetic practices." Instead of the challenge to discover reality and, in communing with it, to find life, Williams writes,

> we are presented with a list of truths for our intellectual assent. . . . And since the devout assume that they possess the truth in the verbalized concepts to which they subscribe, what is called their faith generally makes them insensitive to reality as it is revealed all around them, and deaf to the Eternal Word speaking through all things. For they must ever be cutting it down to size, emptying it of content, so as to make it square with their particular orthodoxy.[2]

Kathleen Norris lays at least part of the blame at the feet of our contemporary therapeutic culture. She writes,

> Modern believers tend to trust in therapy more than mystery—a fact that manifests itself in worship that employs the bland speech of pop psychology and self help, rather than language resonant with poetic meaning.[3]

Dean Sam Miller of Harvard Divinity School, some years ago now, argued that much of the fault lay with the scientific revolution: "Because we are living in an age of exceptional scientific popularity, we have been tempted to use the instruments and means so successful in the laboratory in the field of the spirit. Thus we have tried to sustain the spirit with abstractions, literal creeds, formulas and exact definitions. This pervasive literalness is a blight of death to the soul, and produces only fanaticism and a dubious pharisaical zeal."[4]

"A blight of death to the soul" . . . a dearth of delight. Whatever you might choose to call it, there certainly seems to be a dearth of something in the preaching of our times. And at least two recent Lyman Beecher lecturers have spoken of the state of today's pulpit in somewhat similar terms. Barbara Brown Taylor entitled her 1997 lectures *When God Is Silent* and her three individual lectures "Famine," "Silence," and "Restraint" and said, "This is my reading of our situation at the end of the twentieth century. Our language is broken. There is famine in the land. God's true name can never be spoken."[5]

Just over a decade ago, Walter Brueggemann delivered four lectures on "Numbness and Ache," "Alienation and Rage," "Restlessness and Greed," and "Resistance and Relinquishment"—all of which sounds awfully like a dearth of something. Brueggemann called his entire series *Finally Comes the Poet*,[6] raising all kinds of wild hopes among those few poets who still do try to read theology. Yet, while making a splendid argument for the essential role of poets and poetry in the preaching of today, what we got in the lectures, for better or for worse, what "finally came" was not a poet, at least in those lectures, but an Old Testament professor doing some excellent, if undeniably rather prosy, exegesis. Sad to say, in the field of homiletics, the way is still open, it seems to me, for the arrival, finally and at long last, of the poet.

However, Brueggemann did make the case for poetry, arguing that in a society where the gospel is so widely accepted that it has lost its ability to challenge and to surprise, the church needs an alternative voice, a distinctively different means of communication to renew its age-old message. He called for a mode of speech that is "dramatic, artistic, capable of inviting persons to join in another conversation, free of the reason of technique, unencumbered by ontologies that grow abstract, unembarrassed about concreteness." And thus he challenges us to be "poets that speak against a prose world." Such a poetic mode in preaching, Brueggemann averred, "is not moral instruction or problem solving or doctrinal clarification. It is not good advice, nor is it romantic caressing, nor is it a soothing good humor."[7] The preaching of the poet is rather the disclosing of an alternative vision, of a completely other, and far more radically open-ended portrayal of reality than anything that is currently on offer; than what Brueggemann called "the fearful rationality that keeps the news from being new." He argued:

> The sermon is not normally the place for concrete moral admonition. . . . Nor is the sermon the place for concrete instruction about public policy. . . . The sermon is the place where the church is freed to imagine.[8] . . . The event of preaching is an event in transformed imagination.[9]

The Poetic Vision

What then is this poetic vision Brueggemann seeks to move toward? What might he have had in mind when he hailed the final coming of the poet? In the first place, it has little or nothing to do with explanation, with the logical step-by-step unfolding of mystery, the shedding of light, the solving of problems. Flannery O'Connor is said to have remarked that, far from dissolving all mystery, the task of the novelist—and I would add that of the preacher too—is to deepen mystery. In similar vein, Rubem Alves points out that the verbs "to explain" or "to explicate" come from Latin roots that mean to flatten, to spread out, to make level. He likens our attempts at clarification to the process of earth removal or highway construction:

> A great bulldozer will push the mountains inside the abysses and everything will become a luminous plain under midday sun.[10]

That's what prose is for, after all. The objective of most prose writing is to make things perfectly clear. But there is a realm that lies beyond explanation, a geography of soul and spirit whose heights and depths are beyond any of our calculations or merely logical connections. It was Einstein himself—no stranger to logic and reason— who warned against worshiping the intellect alone, which possesses, he remarked, powerful muscles, but no personality.[11]

T. S. Eliot, speaking of the difficulties of translating poems, told of times when, despite not knowing the meaning of the actual words before him on the page, he nevertheless grasped, or was grasped by the vision of the poet. Eliot suggested that this imaginative communication beyond words was of the essence of poetry: "So in poetry you can, now and then, penetrate into another country, so to speak, before your passport has been issued or your ticket taken."[12]

This urge to explain, this need to make everything perfectly clear, is a pervasive and insistent one. Even my

late colleague and friend Ernest Somerville of First Presbyterian Church, Philadelphia, a prince of preachers notwithstanding, would insist, in a preaching course we
used to teach together, that everything in a sermon had to
be made perfectly clear, or at least as perfectly clear as
possible.

"But Ernest"—I would say to him—"just look around
you; life, death, good and evil, not even to mention love,
all these most vital things are not even semi-perfectly
clear, and as far as I can see they never will be, at least
until the eschaton. We see 'through a glass dimly,' old
friend. So that if we want to talk about such things, we're
going to have to yield a bit on clarity, and lean toward the
language of metaphor and simile, in other words toward
the vision of the poet."

When the critic, in search of clarity, asked the poet,
"What did you want to say?" the poet responded,"I
wanted to say precisely what I did say."[13] Harvard's dis-
tinguished chaplain and Plummer Professor of Christian
Morals, Peter Gomes, puts it this way:

> When I was young I thought my job as a preacher was
> to explain things. In my second ten years of preaching
> I no longer explained, I apologized. In this last third,
> I'm not explaining or apologizing, I'm celebrating the
> holy mysteries of the faith. . . . I depend on metaphor
> rather than metaphysics. We are saved by our
> metaphors, not our metaphysics.[14]

Perhaps another of my poems, a poem I scribbled
down during a pastors' retreat in Ocean City, New Jersey,

can draw some of this together. We had a speaker, I recall, on the topic of silent meditation; and as such speakers tend to do, he went on and on and on. Fortunately we were seated opposite a wide wall of windows that looked out across the boardwalk and beyond, so that, just behind the speaker, one could rest worn and weary eyes upon the Atlantic Ocean in all its vastness.

Two Porpoises Passed By

A pair they made
darkly-matched angled
fins lunging among, across
the blue and sparkling ocean
spread beyond the boardwalk
past the panoramic windows of
our pastors' conference hotel.

We were praying at
the time, striving—closed-eyed—
to lose our stress, find
souls again, and all
in thirty hours or less, before
the plunging back into the daily
mess and management.

My eyes were slitted-open,
unwilling to relinquish that
bright tantalizing scene below,
balm to my sight,
worn down by paper scanning,
the cursor's light green
tracing on the screen.

> And so I caught the deep
> and dreadful brushing-by of mystery,
> exulted, silent, in the moving,
> living presence of an alien world
> that swept along our shores, just as
> it does, and is, in each and every
> moment, whether we watch or pray
> or wake or sleep.[15]

The poetic vision then is a vision ever alert to catch that "deep and dreadful brushing by of mystery" that, despite all our attempts at explanation, accompanies each moment of our living of these days and calls out for our attention. Perhaps the greatest miracle of the Hebrew Scriptures was not the Red Sea crossing after all, but Moses stopping in the wilderness of Horeb, noticing a bush that burned without being burned up, and saying, "I will turn aside and see this great sight." Everything that followed—yes, salvation history itself—hinged upon that one fateful, curious decision: "I will turn aside and see . . ." It happens all the time, you know, if we can only keep our eyes open. Why do we have to close our eyes to pray?

It happens all the time. Oh, not always on quite the scale of Moses' experience in Exodus chapter 3, but the vision, Eliot's passport to another world, is available nevertheless, available at the blink of an eye. A couple of years ago now, while on one of my early morning walks around the village I used to live in—Greenwich Village in Manhattan—I came upon a behemoth of an oil truck making its deliveries. It was a surprisingly elegant rig in shiny two-tone green, and gleaming in three-foot gold lettering along each side of the bulging tank was this one word: MYSTIC. And I stood there gazing at it with a beatific grin. Oh, yes, when I reached the cab, I read there that the rig belonged to the Mystic Oil Co. of Aronimink, New York, but I still cherish that initial astonishment, that glimpse behind the curtain into the absurd—yes at times laughable—mystery that still dogs our every footstep, accompanies our ways with that same delight-filled "wild surmise" John Keats glimpsed within Cortes and his men, "silent upon a peak in Darien."

It is that same mixture of humor and everyday wonder that we meet in Gerard Stern's poem "Peaches":

> What was I thinking of when I threw one of my
> peachstones over the fence at Metro-North,
> and didn't I dream as always it would take
> root in spite of the gravel and the newspaper,
> and wasn't I like that all my life, and who isn't?[16]

So then the poetic vision, as I have called it, is not about explaining, not at all about making things perfectly clear, but about inviting, about evoking, about delighting. It is, as Brueggemann pointed out, less to do with morality, ethics, social concern, right teaching, and more to do with what has been called the central purpose of all Christian ministry, "the mediation of transcendence," a mediation out of which, once achieved, all these other necessary concerns must follow. "Seek ye first the kingdom of God . . . and all these things shall be added unto you." (Matt. 6:33 KJV)

Apprehend God In All Things . . .

But there is more involved here than some vague and generalized experience of transcendence. Moses may have been intrigued by the strangeness of that bush, but he was transformed and empowered by the presence in and through that bush—I'm tempted to adapt the old definition of a sacrament here and say, "in, with, and under"—he was transformed by the presence he encountered there of the Maker of heaven and earth.

"The creation, preservation and government of the universe" is how the Belgic Confession of 1561 puts it:

> We know God by the creation, preservation and government of the universe: which is before our eyes as a most elegant book, wherein all creatures, great and small, are as so many characters leading us to contemplate the invisible things of God, namely, his eternal power and Godhead.

This echoes Meister Eckhart, who wrote:

> Apprehend God in all things,
> For God is in all things.
> Every single creature is full of God
> And is a book about God.
> Every creature is a Word of God.[17]

While John Keble, the 19th-century English poet, reminds us in his hymn:

> There is a book who runs may read,
>   Which heavenly truth imparts;
> And all the lore its scholars need,
>   Pure eyes and Christian hearts.

The works of God above, below,
    Within us and around,
Are pages in that book to show
    How God himself is found. . . .

Thou who hast given me eyes to see
    And love this sight so fair,
Give me a heart to find out thee,
    And read thee everywhere.[18]

In our own time, Richard Wilbur choreographs this vision into exquisite poetic form in his poem "Mayflies": glimpsing the great circle dance of the universe in the seemingly ordinary ephemeral shimmer of a cloud of mayflies caught in the rays of the setting sun; then moving from intimations of his own mortality, to the poet's glad calling to witness to the glory of the One who is the caller, the great caller of the cosmic dance.

Mayflies

In sombre forest, when the sun was low,
I saw from unseen pools a mist of flies
    In their quadrillions rise
And animate a ragged patch of glow
With sudden glittering—as when a crowd
    of stars appear
Through a brief gap in black and driven cloud,
One arc of their great round-dance showing clear.

It was no muddled swarm I witnessed, for
In entrechats each fluttering insect there
    Rose two steep yards in air,
Then slowly floated down to climb once more,

17

So that they all composed a manifold
    And figured scene,
And seemed the weavers of some cloth of gold,
Or the fine pistons of some bright machine.

Watching those lifelong dancers of a day
As night closed in, I felt myself alone
    In a life too much my own,
More mortal in my separateness than they—
Unless, I thought, I had been called to be
    Not fly or star
But one whose task is joyfully to see
How fair the fiats of the caller are.[19]

The poet, and surely the preacher too, is one called to be

    Not fly or star
But one whose task is joyfully to see
How fair the fiats of the caller are.

The master, of course, of such poetry of divine imma-
nence, such a truly sacramental view of the universe, is
Gerard Manley Hopkins, whose dazzlingly intricate verse
first captured my own imagination at Yale in Julian
Hartt's course "Christianity in Contemporary Culture."
Hopkins's vision is of a world in which the hand of the
Maker, and of the Redeemer too, is to be glimpsed just
beneath the surface, not only of the world of nature, but
of events and personalities as well. There is a point in
almost every Hopkins poem in which the veil is lifted, the
screen is removed, and the reality of God breaks through
like the sun, which has been there all the time, emerging
from behind a layer of cloud. David Daiches in his 1983
Gifford Lectures, "God and the Poets," observes of the
presence of the divine in Hopkins's poetry: "God—and

this is true in all of Hopkins's poems—is never a *deus ex machina*, because Hopkins through his idiom and imagery makes clear that God only emerges because he has been there all the time."[20]

Watch for this now in his sublime sonnet, as the poet discovers the risen Christ disclosed in and through everything and everyone.

> As kingfishers catch fire, dragonflies draw flame;
> As tumbled over rim in roundy wells
> Stones ring; like each tucked string tells, each hung bell's
> Bow swung finds tongue to fling out broad its name;
> Each mortal thing does one thing and the same:
> Deals out that being indoors each one dwells;
> Selves—goes itself; *myself* it speaks and spells,
> Crying *What I do is me: for that I came.*
>
> I say more: the just man justices;
> Keeps grace: that keeps all his goings graces;
> Acts in God's eye what in God's eye he is—
> Christ—for Christ plays in ten thousand places,
> Lovely in limbs, and lovely in eyes not his
> To the Father through the features of men's faces.[21]

Or see this again in what is perhaps Hopkins's best-known poem, "The Windhover: To Christ Our Lord," where the word "Buckle!" marks the crux, the point at which the poem literally breaks open to reveal, in the plunging hawk, the glory of Christ, his "chevalier."

> Brute beauty and valour and act, oh, air, pride, plume here
>   Buckle! AND the fire that breaks from thee then, a
>   billion
> Times told lovelier, more dangerous, O my chevalier![22]

A couple of springs ago now, while visiting family in the north of England, my cousin insisted that I visit a nearby "bluebell wood," dimly remembered from childhood. The tiny low flowers covered the ground like a sky-blue mist floating among the tree trunks, almost as if the heavens above had also swept, momentarily at least, beneath our feet to enfold us in an azure springtime ecstasy of bright, essential blueness. The scene recalled for me a page in Hopkins's diary where, alongside a detailed drawing and description of a bluebell, he wrote, "I do not think I have ever seen anything more beautiful than the bluebell I have been looking at. I know the beauty of our Lord by it."[23]

As a Scot, of course, I would be remiss indeed if I did not at least mention here the immense contribution of Celtic Christianity to this ancient vision of the presence of God in all created things. On my study desk in Maine, where I have done most of the preparatory work for this book, there sits a miniature Celtic cross, a reproduction actually of the towering stone Saint Martin's cross which stands outside the abbey on Iona. And right there, with its arms embracing the wide circle of the world, and its surface encrusted with, to us, bizarre designs of mythical beasts, semihuman figures and plant patterns, a historic claim is still being made: not just that the world and all its creatures belong to God, but also that the God who saves on the cross is also the God who creates, and that this God is to be encountered through all the rich variety and wonder of this creation we experience as reality.

Keeping All of Reality in View

Reality, however, involves more than Celtic abbeys, king-fishers, dragonflies, and starry skies. It also includes war-fare, disaster, the full range of what Scotland's bard, Robert Burns, termed "man's inhumanity to man." And if this poetic vision I have been describing was unable to glimpse the divine presence also in these equally real experiences and phenomena, then it would be a severely, perhaps even fatally, limited vision.

Several years ago, when we moved from tiny, idyllic Swarthmore, Pennsylvania, to the heart of New York City to take up my new ministry at the First Presbyterian Church there, I wondered about that; wondered what the rather drastic change of environment might do to the poetry I wrote, to my entire experience of God's presence in creation It must be said that the adjustment was truly difficult at first, I felt as if I had moved, not just to a different world, but to a different planet. But by my second Easter in Manhattan, the vision had been firmly renewed, and had found expression in a new poem, "Holy Satur-day at the Green Market." The poem is set in New York on the day before Easter, at the Union Square Green Mar-ket, a place where farmers, beekeepers, wine and bread and cheese makers, sheepherders, fishermen too, sell their own fresh produce direct to city dwellers—a place, three city blocks from our apartment, that Mhairi, my wife, and I would visit Saturday mornings to select the makings of our evening meal:

Holy Saturday at the Green Market

I think I caught the risen Christ,
just yesterday, on Broadway alongside Union Square.
We were returning from the Green Market
—fresh fish, green mesclun with a pinch
of bright and edible nasturtiums tossed on top,
some tiny new potatoes for our evening meal—
when I glimpsed ahead a shambling, awkward figure
lurching his twisted way along the sidewalk
and jerking fiercely now and then as if in seizure.
He wore a red baseball cap slightly off center,
sweatshirt, jeans, sneakers—all shabby
but well cared for, clean—and over his right arm
a cardboard carton with the lid cut off to shape
a sort of basket, I suppose, to display wares.
I glanced in as we passed, and sure enough
there were ballpoint pens, other plastic items
in there waiting to be purchased. Silent—
in my head—I wondered at the courage of one
so violently deformed, yet coping, contriving
to survive this predatory city.

Those contorted legs could not move him
that fast, and we were swiftly past him to confront,
lying across a heap of trash bags up against the wall,
a homeless man, asleep, with the usual pathetic sign
informing all and sundry:
    I'm in trouble, please help. Someday
    I may be able to do the same for you.
I walked on, ignored both plea and promise,
passed right by as I've been taught to
by this casual, careless, care-less cruel city;
then glancing back over my shoulder saw our friend
in the red baseball cap struggle across,
laboriously read—how long it seemed to take—

that grubby and ill-lettered sign, then lean
over and drop something in the cup.

Yes, I realize, it only encourages. I know
they'll likely spend it all on booze. I've heard
and lived these arguments, knowing far too much,
believing far too little, and being so afraid,
for years now. But there was something in
that simple act; an eastered innocence
put me to shame, drove me to my knees
among the sidewalk lily vendors.
I think I caught the risen Christ,
a day early, but there just the same,
on Broadway yesterday alongside Union Square.[24]

A Further Challenge

On September 11, 2001, that vision was put to an infinitely more severe test as the First Presbyterian Church in the City of New York, my former congregation (I retired in 2000), lost eight members of her family at the World Trade Center. These were folk I had welcomed into the church and worked and worshiped with throughout the varied life of a busy urban congregation. I traveled back to the city shortly afterward to preach at the funeral of one of those killed—a young wife and mother of two children—and earlier in the day I made the pilgrimage downtown to visit The Site . . . Ground Zero, as it had already come to be known. I was wearing my clerical collar in preparation for the afternoon funeral, and that, plus my ID, was sufficient to get me through the National Guard barricades, past the gas-masked soldiers—the dust and smoke were still horrendous—and into Saint Paul's Chapel, the historic sanctuary that had miraculously survived right on the edge of the abyss. I had prayed there and attended concerts in earlier, different times, but on that day I entered a transformed, scarcely recognizable space. This poem, "A Visit to Saint Paul's Chapel," attempts to relate what I found.

A Visit to Saint Paul's Chapel

PORT-A-JOHNS—some thirty of them—
line the foot of the church steps,
facing outward onto Broadway.
The elegant pillared portico is become
a gratis cafeteria; hot soup, sandwiches, soda,
all kinds of fruit, cakes and candy,
with chairs and tables set in sunlight
and rescue workers, soldiers, police officers,
and volunteers relaxing and eating together.
Almost a holiday scene, except for the dust,
the heavy, clinging smell of burning,
and the absence of laughter.

Inside, the historic pews are furnished
with blankets, quilts, and pillows
while the side aisles overflow with toiletries.
A grand piano stands smothered in stuffed animal toys.
The entire sacred space festooned with banners:
    TO NEW YORK AND ALL ITS RESCUERS
    KEEP YOUR SPIRITS UP
    OKLAHOMA LOVES YOU!!
hangs from a balcony, while on a pillar:
    YOU RAN IN WHEN
    WE ALL RAN OUT.

FOR THAT WE ARE FOREVER GRATEFUL.
GOD BLESS BM LADDER 20.
A letter in the pew rack from a choirgirl in Tucson says:
    I wanted you to know that you had a friend
    in Tucson who was praying for you.

MASSAGE THERAPY, reads a sign in one corner,
CHIROPRACTORS occupy another.
The proud George Washington pew is filled
with podiatrists under FOOT CARE. Along the rear,
on the very brink of hell, stretches a rack of solid work-
    boots.
"The wreckage and intense heat shred the workers' foot-
    gear."
said my volunteer escort/guide from Asheville, NC.
A noontime prayer service begins.
"The self-satisfied bromides of organized religion,"
as one sophisticated critic said recently on NPR.
Twenty or so unsophisticated rescue workers,
National Guard troops, and peace officers
stand to pray and listen for Good News,
still others simply sleep.
et lux in tenebris lucet—
and the darkness has not overcome it.[25]

Today, as I write these words with the drums of war hammering ever louder, and the death toll from that calamitous event and its seemingly unending aftermath mounting by the day, even the hour, the creative imagination is still active, and even more vibrant and vital. My fellow Presbyterian poet and dear friend Ann Barr Weems wrote the following poem in response to an invitation from the Presbyterian Peace Fellowship, a poem that was

read as a prayer at the fellowship's gathering during the
2004 General Assembly in Richmond, Virginia.

Peace, Peace . . .

The world has become the valley of the shadow of death,
but we who believe are asked to walk it without fear,
asked to remember that our Shepherd will not leave us.
We're up to our hearts in the daily death count,
blood spurting at us from our televisions,
and leaving our hands smeared
when we read the morning paper.
All over the world the Children of God
are killing one another,
and the bands play and the
flag-draped bodies come home,
and God is invoked to bless it all.
Peace, Peace, but there is no peace. . . .
The killing and the maiming continue.

The world sits in the Chair of Despair,
dismissing those who preach peace.
"Dreamers!" they shout,
and somehow "dreamers"
sounds like a curse word,
as the word "Peace"
sounds unpatriotic while
the word "War" sounds
strong and mighty. . . .
Righteous and just,
and godly.

There is no sanctuary
for those who preach peace,
for patriotism trumps faith,
and besides the church is busy

with its own quarreling.
Too busy for peace. . . .
Too busy for peace. . . .
There is no sanctuary
for those who seek peace
except in the word of God,
except in the heart of God.

In the word of God
we find the Prince of Peace
who today walks through the blood
and picks up his sheep in his arms,
one by one,
and takes them home.
Then he turns and strides into
our church sanctuaries,
right down the carpeted aisles,
ignoring the blood on his sandals,
and stands before the church
and says, "Follow me."
We'll be there soon, we answer,
just as soon as we finish our quarreling.
"Love one another." says
The Prince of Peace,
those bloody sandals trying
to walk into our hearts.
But the church is terribly busy
with its own quarreling.
No, there is no sanctuary,
for those who preach peace.
But those who preach peace
know we do not have to
apologize for preaching
peace in the church of
Jesus Christ.

Peace, peace, there is no peace.
The world shakes its head
at protest and prayer.
"Dreamers!"
They scream again,
but those who preach peace
know that peace is not a dream.
Peace is a promise.
Peace is a promise from the heart of God
to our hearts.
Go now in the promise of peace.
Go now knowing that this church
and this world belong to the Prince of Peace
no matter what
no matter what.

No matter what, feed his sheep.
No matter what, love one another.
No matter what, preach peace
in the assembly of the world
and the assembly of the church.
No matter what, believe that
Peace will come,
for peace is not a dream.
Peace is a promise.
Go now to tell the others.
Go now to shout it from the roof tops.
Shout it in the name of Jesus,
Jesus, the Prince of Peace. Amen.[26]

Creation as Sacrament

The poetic vision, then, the gift of creative imagination, is
essential to all we have to say in the pulpit—the long-

neglected source, I am convinced, of genuine renewal and refreshment for preaching in our times. "Sacramental" is a word frequently used to describe this whole imaginative process of disclosing God's presence in creation. While some may question this undoubted broadening of a concept central and essential to the experience of Christian worship, it seems to me that is precisely what I and countless others have been doing all along. In worship we take representative elements of the daily stuff of existence—water, bread and wine—and, by means of words and gestures, silences too, reveal within them their innate holiness, the living grace and glory of the divine. But just as the content of the sermon is worthless until it is applied to life beyond the sanctuary doors, so this experience of the elevation of the ordinary needs to be extended far beyond the altar and communion table, throughout the entire creation, until the fullest range of reality is broken open like a sacramental loaf, to disclose the nurturing, inviting, welcoming grace that hides within. My poem "Broad-Cast" hints at just such a widening of the sacramental:

Broad-Cast
Strange
How bread
In breaking
Spreads
Shares
Itself divides
Distributes crumbs
All sundry

> Take
> Care your
> Fair white linen
> Not confine
> The scattered seed
> To virgin soil
> Or all too narrow
> Furrow[27]

Such a potentially all-embracing vision will ultimately discover, not just God through the lens of reality, but reality through the lens that is God. Or as Saint John of the Cross put it, "And here is the remarkable delight of this awakening: the soul knows creatures through God and not God through creatures."[28]

Surely here, in the sacramental dimension of all of creation, we glimpse a vision and perspective not only to be sought after by the preacher, but to be communicated with true grace and sheer delight to all who come to us hungry for a glimpse of an alternative universe where there are many ways of knowing, where one sees with the heart as well as with the eye, and where the next intriguing clues in the celestial treasure hunt lie just around the corner. For,

> Eye hath not seen, nor ear heard,
> Nor have entered into the heart of man
> the things which God hath prepared for them that love
> him.
> But God hath revealed them unto us by his Spirit.
> For the Spirit searcheth all things, yea, the deep things of
> God.

Flirting or Courting

One of the most constant sources of delight and alternative vision over my now-forty years of ordained ministry has been the writings of my Presbyterian clergy colleague and friend Frederick Buechner. I close this chapter with an excerpt from his book *Brendan,* an excerpt that itself portrays something of the art I am calling for. Saint Brendan, as a young man, is traveling across Ireland with his friend Finn, and preaching the gospel to the people he encounters on the way. Finn takes up the narrative:

> They was poor folk mostly. They'd be gathering white-stalked wild garlic or nuts as might be or grazing their bony cows on some common pasturage. He'd give them a bit to eat out of our plump sacks and tell them news of Christ like it was no older than a day. Nor did he tell it with gull eyes like Jarlath nor grinding it down to a fine dust like Erc. He'd make them laugh instead at how Christ gulled the elders out of stoning to death the woman caught in the act of darkness. He'd drop their jaws telling them how he hailed Lazarus out of his green grave and walked on water without making holes. He'd bring a mist to their eyes spinning out the holy words Christ said on the hill and telling them the way he shared his last loaf with his friends the night the bullies come for him in the garden.
>
> It was like flirting or courting the way Brendan did it. He'd tease them along till they was hot for more and then skitter off saying he'd be back one day soon or another like him to tell them another tale or two if they'd mend their ways in the meantime.[29]

"... like flirting or courting ..." What a splendid, and startlingly fresh image for the calling we share in the pulpit! Next time you sit down in your study before your trusty word processor and turn your thoughts toward Sunday morning, try reaching back to those exhilarating, humiliating days of courtship, no matter how near or far. And then do your best to recapture something of their sheer delight, of the comedy and agony, the joy and despair, the fervor and foolishness too, of that time of all times. Then get it into your sermon. Maybe they'll even want to come back and hear you again.

Chapter 2

AN IMAGINING GOD

❧❧❧❧

I have yet many things to say to you,
but you cannot bear them now.
When the Spirit of truth comes,
he will guide you into all the truth. . . .
He will take what is mine and declare it to you.
                                John 16:12, 15 RSV

George Bernard Shaw, that consummate imaginer, in his
play, *Saint Joan*, has Joan say, at one point, "I hear voices
telling me what to do. They come from God." Captain
Robert, Squire of Baudricourt, whose aid Joan is seeking
to enlist, answers scornfully, "They come from your
imagination." Joan replies, "Of course. That is how the
message of God comes to us."[1]

   Is imagination, creativity, then—in an attitude which
I deplored in chapter 1—an optional extra to be used or
ignored by the preacher at will? Is it to be regarded as a
piece of trim, an item of decor, an occasional alternative
approach for preachers who happen to be that way
inclined? Or might it rather be, as I have been proposing,
the essential foundation for proclamation, that vital
ingredient without which preaching becomes the dry as

dust—ashes to ashes, dust to dust—dreary recitation of long moribund theories, doctrines, popular nostrums?

Henry Ward Beecher back in 1872, inaugurating the lectureship named for his illustrious father, Lyman Beecher, recognized this primary importance of the imagination:

> [T]he first element on which your preaching will largely depend for power and success, you will perhaps be surprised to learn, is *Imagination*, which I regard as the most important of all the elements that go to make the preacher.[2]

And later he comments:

> The imagination offers one of the most instructive sides of the mind. It is one of the sides through which knowledge can best come to men: it is employed throughout the scriptures, eminently, as a vehicle for imparting knowledge.[3]

Yet even Beecher, in his day, had to admit that his enthusiasm for the imagination was not exactly widely shared. "Theologians," he acknowledged, "are accustomed to speak of the imagination as though a taint rested upon it."[4] While John Baillie, in his book *Our Knowledge of God*, put it this way:

> I have long been of opinion that the part played by the imagination in the soul's dealings with God, though it has always been understood by those skilled in the practice of the Christian cure of souls, has never been given proper place in Christian theology, which has too much been ruled by intellectualistic preconceptions.[5]

Even a cursory acquaintance with the history of Christian thought would bear this out. The Christian tradition, on the whole, has tended to stand firmly on the side of Squire Robert, Saint Joan's adversary, in nurturing a deep suspicion of creativity and all that it encompasses. The tale, I suspect, is a familiar one of the influential cardinal, offended by the "full frontal nudity" of Michelangelo's figures in the Sistine Chapel's "Last Judgment," who organized what became known as the "Fig Leaf Campaign" to have the figures covered. The censorship eventually succeeded; but the artist's revenge is to be seen to this day in the section of the ceiling that portrays the darkest corner of hell, where the cardinal himself is clearly depicted as Minos, judge of the underworld, fully clothed and frying forever.[6]

The classic *Book of Common Prayer* of the Church of England, for all its own imaginative and elegant use of the English language, never fails to warn us against what it calls "the evil imaginations of our hearts." And both Luther and Calvin, throughout the Reformation period, issued forth regular denunciations of any human attempt to bring the imagination to bear upon issues of theology or biblical interpretation. Although, as Tom Troeger comments in his book *Imagining a Sermon*, "If the power of God's grace is as magnificent as the Protestant Reformers claimed, then (surely) grace can redeem even the corruptions of the human imagination." And he adds, "Neither Luther nor Calvin considers how his own imagination is engaged in the creation of his theology."[7]

The Scots too, for all their aforementioned deep and rich

heritage in Celtic spirituality, have long shared this deep suspicion. That same Saint Martin's Cross I described in the previous chapter, embossed upon my Church of Scotland *Book of Common Order*, got me into considerable hot water some years ago with my wife Mhairi's Great Aunt Tina, an enormous and truly formidable retired governess who was accompanying us on a Scottish pulpit supply trip one Sunday morning. Catching sight of my little book as she squeezed herself into the car, she pointed to the cross embossed on the cover and inquired haughtily, "What, may I inquire, is that?" "It's a symbol, Great Aunt Tina," I responded defensively. "Harrumph . . ." she replied, "I thought we did away with symbolism years ago."

Even in the Scriptures it can be a challenge to find much that is in any way positive concerning the imagination. Back at the beginning, for example, in the prologue to the flood narrative, we read, "The LORD saw that the wickedness of man was great in the earth, and that every imagination of the thoughts of his heart was only evil continually" (Gen. 6:5 RSV). It's hard to get more definite, more categorical, than that:

. . . that *every* imagination was *only* evil *continually.*

Indeed, much of the ongoing suspicion and mistrust between the ecclesiastical and the artistic communities—and I used to run up against this in my congregation in Greenwich Village all the time—is rooted in this biblical ambivalence concerning the imagination, that sees it not so much as a gift, but as a curse or, at the very least, a source of dire temptation.

Yet, granted all this, I am convinced that there is also available, within that same biblical and theological tradition, an alternative understanding, even a reading of basic doctrines, that lays the foundation for all that I am trying to elucidate in this book, and that supports my advocacy of the indispensable role of creativity and imagination in preaching. It is that alternative understanding that I will seek to spell out in the remainder of this chapter.

The Divine Imagination

> I have yet many things to say to you,
> but you cannot bear them now.
> When the Spirit of truth comes,
> he will guide you into all the truth. . . .
> He will take what is mine and declare it to you.

Theologically, I begin not with our human imagination but with God's, with the creativity of the Almighty; for in that same book of Genesis in which is found the categorical condemnation I cited above in Genesis 6—in fact, at the very beginning of that book—it is specifically and exclusively as Creator that we first encounter the divinity. This is the one who, out of some eternal desire of Love for a beloved—out of the inherent, intrinsic necessity for Love to express itself, bestow itself, pour itself out—imagines, and then creates, permits to exist—"Let there be . . . and there was . . ."—the entire gamut, the radiant spectrum of creation that we find described in Genesis chapter 1. This is the one who was, as Cheryl Forbes daringly expresses it, "the first and only person to imagine anything without the aid of memory or prior experience."[8]

This is the one who, out of absolutely nothing, conceives, and then creates, absolutely everything. Kenneth Patchen's whimsical little poem captures something of the sheer exuberance, the imaginative freedom that must have been involved:

> Elephants and eskimos are the sort of inventions
> makes me sure God has a couple
> three-four kids of his own.[9]

After all, it's not *every* day one comes up with a universe! Imagine that, if you can! Patchen's recognition of the dimension of play within the act of creation is hardly without theological precedent. In the Scriptures themselves we read that when God "laid the foundations of the earth,"

> the morning stars sang together
> and all the heavenly beings shouted for joy.
> Job 38:4, 7 NRSV

While Sophia—Lady Wisdom—in Proverbs surely danced a highland fling of sheer delight when she witnessed all created things as they came into being. Hear how Eugene Peterson translates Proverbs 8:29–31:

> When he drew a boundary for Sea,
>   posted a sign that said, NO TRESPASSING,
> And then staked out Earth's foundations,
>   I was right there with him, making sure everything fit.
> Day after day I was there, with my joyful applause,
>   always enjoying his company,
> Delighted with the world of things and creatures,
>   Happily celebrating the human family.[10]

In my poem "Imago" I make my own playful attempt at the creation story.

Imago
With you it's all
"no sooner said than done,"
or so the Book informs us.
    "Let there be . . ."
you said; and then there was.
Things came to be just like that.
But surely even you must daydream now
and then, fool around (a holy fool, of course)
with one idea and then another, and another,
let your imagination conjure up
(again I mean a holy magic)
a whole raft of possibilities, alternatives,
even the odd outright impossibility
(after all, with you all things . . .).
I suspect that your original celestial imagining
must have come up with twists and turns,
and even problems, that brought on a holy grin,
perhaps even a belly laugh or two,
or where is all the fun in it?
Why bother?[11]

Willliam Muehl, in his insightful book *Why Preach? Why Listen?* (based on his 1984–85 Beecher Lectures), argues that this image of God as Creator—an image still cherished in Eastern Christianity while consistently neglected in the West—must be the preeminent image for our time. The entire message of the book of Job, not to mention the Psalms, is that while God may also be a God of justice and of compassion, God's creativity reigns paramount and, when necessary, takes priority over these and every other attribute of the divine. Muehl writes:

> If one takes the Hebrew Scriptures seriously and regards them as something more than a grace note en route to the Nunc Dimittis, one thing becomes inescapably clear. The God of the Bible is before all else and above all else the Creating One, the one *by whom all things are made* and without whom nothing is made that was made.[12]

As for justice and compassion, those attributes of God that command so much homiletical attention in our day, Muehl says:

> If the divine purpose for humanity is justice, it is obviously very poorly administered. And speaking from this perspective one of Elie Wiesel's characters, a learned rabbi, cries angrily in the face of a pogrom, "On the day of judgement God will have much to answer for!"
>
> If, on the other hand, God's primary concern is works of mercy, honest people must ask *why* this painful mess called history was ever allowed to come into being in the first place.
>
> It is the creative purpose of God, enshrined in the very atoms of our bodies, a purpose which, in order to fulfil itself in time, must cut ruthlessly across every finite value; it is only this creating purpose that can nerve us to live with some measure of joy even in the midst of suffering.[13]

I am reminded of the close of Archibald MacLeish's play *JB* when Sarah, Job's wife, cradling a newly budded forsythia branch she has found growing among the ashes, tells her husband, "You wanted justice, didn't you? There isn't any. There's the world." Ann Carson's poem "God's Justice" expresses something of this same perspective, along with a touch of sheer delight.

God's Justice

In the beginning there were days set aside for various
    tasks.
On the day He was to create justice
God got involved in making a dragonfly

and lost track of time.
It was about two inches long
with turquoise dots all the way down its back like Lauren
    Bacall.
God watched it bend its tiny wire elbows
as it set about cleaning the transparent case of its head.
The eye globes mounted on the case

rotated this way and that
as it polished every angle.
Inside the case

which was glassy black like the windows of a
    downtown bank
God could see the machinery humming
and He watched the hum

travel all the way down turquoise dots to the end of the
    tail
and breathe off as light.
Its black wings vibrated in and out.[14]

Creativity, then, the work of the imagination, begins with God and is essential, quintessential, indeed, to God's

41

nature. It is what God preeminently does. God is the Great Imaginer.

The Human Imagination

> I have yet many things to say to you,
> but you cannot bear them now.
> When the Spirit of truth comes,
> he will guide you into all the truth. . . .
> He will take what is mine and declare it to you.

When it comes to humanity—what used in less enlightened days to be called the doctrine of man—the reality does not change. As God is primarily the Creator, so God's creation, humankind, is called to create, not merely called to be the object or the product of the divine imagination, but called to be a participant *in* that creative imagination. Muehl puts it this way: "And when humanity appears on the scene it does so as the instrument of (God's) continuing creativity."[15]

This calling is spelled out in both of the Genesis creation stories. The charge to woman and man to "be fruitful and multiply, and fill the earth and subdue it" (Gen. 1:28 RSV) and Adam's participation in the naming of the animals—this conferring upon God's newly formed creatures of no mere label, but the very essence of their identity (Gen. 2: 18–20)—make this instrumentality perfectly clear. And from the formation of these biblical creation narratives to this day, any number of scholars and artists have explored this fertile link between God's creativity and our own.

The Orthodox theologian Nikolai Berdyaev writes persuasively of God's demand that humanity participate in God's creation. In his major work, *The Destiny of Man* he writes, "Christ condemned the burying of a talent in the earth, i.e. the lack of creativeness. The whole of Saint Paul's teaching about various gifts is teaching about man's creative calling. Gifts are from God and they indicate a call to creativity."[16]

Berdyaev clearly underlines the imperative note in God's call to create. It is not only an invitation, certainly not merely an option. It is "God's demand." In *The Meaning of the Creative Act*, he urges, "True creativity is theurgy, God-activity, activity together with God."[17] C. S. Lewis, in his *Letters to Malcolm*, looks at this "demand" from God's own point of view and in the light of God's own nature:

> Creation seems to be delegation through and through. He will do nothing simply of Himself which can be done by creatures. I suppose this is because He is a giver. And He has nothing to give but Himself. And to give Himself is to do His deeds—in a sense, and on varying levels to be Himself—through the things He has made.[18]

Among the artists, Archibald MacLeish, again, echoes the opening verses of Genesis as he speaks for all creators and imaginers—poets and preachers too—describing the poetic task as "struggling with non-being to force it to yield Being." And that same creative struggle can be seen reflected in the entire human enterprise of the arts as writers, painters, sculptors, composers have wrestled to shape meaning from the inchoate mass of reality. In this light, perhaps it is no accident that one of the earliest schools of Scottish poets was called "the Makars"—the Makers. In fact the Greek word *poietes* from which our word "poet" derives has the double meaning of both "maker" and "poet."

Staying with Genesis, however, I find the roots of this "call to create" identified most powerfully in the biblical understanding of the *imago Dei,* that Maker's mark of the divine imprinted upon us, implanted into us from the beginning.

> Then God said, "Let us make humankind in our image, according to our likeness; and let them have dominion over the fish of the sea, and over the birds of the air, and over the cattle, and over all the wild animals of the earth, and over every creeping thing that creeps upon the earth." So God created humankind in his image, in the image of God he created them; male and female he created them. (Gen. 1:26–27 NRSV)

Surely if one were to inquire in what, precisely, that foundational image consisted, the reponse, given the context, would be reasonably obvious. It was, and is, the image of the Creator, the maker, molder and giver of life. Thus, if the image of God within us identifies who we essentially are, then we are essentially creators, cocreators with God, formers and shapers and expressers of reality, those who, through the divine image embedded at the core of our being, confer life, and form and meaning upon the chaotic primary stuff of existence. We are, in fact, most like to God, most Godlike—and also most fully our own selves, most fully human, most fulfilled—when we are involved in the act of creation.

In just such a spirit, that of seeking out the *imago Dei* in every field and endeavor of life, almost forty years ago we inaugurated what we hoped would be an annual arts festival at Yale Divinity School. For one weekend in the spring, students, faculty, and friends celebrated the human imagination as expressed in the arts. A play was produced; I still remember memorizing line after line of meaningless mumbo jumbo as the Professor in Ionesco's play *The Lesson*. There were a coffee house and cabaret, concerts, poetry and prose readings, art and sculpture exhibits, dance; and the point was, we did all this, not just to liven things up, or to show the other graduate schools that we could do it too (although I'll never forget several earnest Yale Drama School types inquiring about my use of the techniques of Stanislavsky, who I then suspected was some mystical Eastern Orthodox theologian). But our point was not to act sophisticated but to insist, in as imaginative a way as possible, that the religious vision and the artistic vision were one, and that the same creator God was at work—or better, at play—in both arenas.

Dorothy L. Sayers, creator of the Lord Peter Wimsey mystery novels as well as of powerful religious drama and literary scholarship, goes even further, and sees the human imagination not just as a means of working together with God, but also as an avenue, or perhaps a window, into the being of God's own self. After all, if the imagination represents the image of the divine within us, then our imagination, investigated imaginatively, should reveal at least an outline of the One whose image it is. In a tantalizing approach to the Trinity, Sayers traces the progressive modes of an idea, which arises spontaneously, created ex nihilo in the mind of the artist; is expressed (incarnated) in an actual drama; and then becomes somehow incorporated—mediated by the Spirit—into the minds and lives of the audience who witness the play.

Yet another imaginative approach to the Trinity—and, to be sure, we can use as many of these as we can find—adopts the imagery, not of the theatre this time, but of the dance.[19] At the close of the *Divine Comedy*, Canto 36 of *The Paradiso*, Dante sees a dazzling vision of the three persons of the Trinity as three moving circles in one and the same orbit, somewhat reminiscent of that great circle dance evoked in Richard Wilbur's poem "Mayflies": "In the profound and shining being of the deep light appeared to me three circles, of three colours, and one magnitude."[20]

The love that is the motive force moving in divine *perichoresis* around and between the three spheres is also the power that turns the great stately gavotte of the galaxies and the delicate minuet of the molecules and atoms. In Dante's closing words, "To the high fantasy here power failed; but already my desire and will were rolled—even as a wheel that moveth equally—by the Love that moves the sun and the other stars."[21]

My poem "Cosmicology" is an attempt to express my own experience of the wonder inherent in this difficult, yet delightful doctrine.

Cosmicology

On the outskirts of the Father
turns the Son, swirling clouds
that overlap without colliding,
bleeding sparks that soar
beyond the Milky Way,
spins the Spirit flaming
in an vast encompassing caress
that shawls itself about all three,
sweeps forth again in flagrant rays
of blazing tenderness and grace
to touch and bless, embrace,
the furthest nearest fringes of eternity.[22]

Teilhard de Chardin, using somewhat similar imagery, roots this action of the Trinity right back again within the life of humanity: "By means of all created things, without exception, the divine assails us, penetrates us and moulds us. We imagined it as distant and inaccessible, whereas in fact we live steeped in its burning layers. *In eo vivimus.*"[23]

Incarnation—Further Implications

I have yet many things to say to you,
but you cannot bear them now.
When the Spirit of truth comes,
he will guide you into all the truth. . . .
He will take what is mine and declare it to you.

The traditional doctrine of incarnation provides another way to undergird theologically what I have called the poetic vision, the work of the imagination. Perhaps the most telling, and certainly the most concise, comment I have seen recently on the incarnation was made by one of Patrick Henry's students and is recorded in Henry's fascinating book *The Ironic Christian's Companion:*

> If God had wanted to appeal directly to our minds, Mary would have written a book instead of bearing a child.[24]

Incarnation as a concept has traditionally been interpreted as a vehicle by means of which one might reveal previously unknown truths about the nature of God and God's limitless, indomitable grace. However, from a more terrestrial perspective, the incarnation also tells us much about the creation itself, this world into which God in Christ is born. For once the divine has been born into and become part and parcel of the daily round of human existence, then this human existence, and every blessed element of it, has become hallowed in a new and infinitely rich way. The holy has entered the ordinary, and the ordinary can never be the same again. In the light of Bethlehem's manger, not only sacred places, holy moments, but this entire world has been invaded, and is pervaded through and through with the presence and the power of divinity, and specifically with the reality—dare we say (once again borrowing the language of the Sacrament) the "real presence"—of the risen Christ.

We have already seen, in Gerard Manley Hopkins's sonnet in chapter 1, how Christ is to be glimpsed—more than glimpsed, encountered—in the way that all created things, dragonflies, stones dropped into roundy wells, sounding bells, yes, and windhovers too, act out their essence, simply be themselves, and how, at the close, he is most fully seen as he

> ... plays in ten thousand places,
> Lovely in limbs, and lovely in eyes not his
> To the Father through the features of men's faces.[25]

Did you read not long ago of the Ugandan doctor who insisted—against all prudent counsel and the interests of his own young wife and family—on staying on in his hospital during a savage outbreak of the Ebola virus to treat the onslaught of victims there? He died, of course, another victim to the virus, along with many of his health workers, and gave his life in being, in Hopkins's terms, fully his own self, in living out the essence of what and who he was, in other words, in healing and saving others.

Another poem of mine, simply called "Real Presence," evokes this idea of ongoing incarnation, on this occasion at the Gay Pride parade in New York City. Soon after our move to the city, my congregation participated in that event for the first time by providing a water table—a series of tables actually, and massive urns, set up outside the church doors along Fifth Avenue—from which they offered a cup of cold water in Christ's name to those who marched by. It was a significant witness because, situated as we were near the end of the route, the hot and weary marchers would have passed many houses of worship along the length of Fifth Avenue, seeing only locked gates and doors or, as at Saint Patrick's Cathedral, barricades and a massive police presence. The parade came

right after Sunday morning service, and so I was there in
my "official capacity," in full clerical garb.

Real Presence

Yes, a frilly pink tutu
was, more or less—more less
than more—all he wore,
that and a tall pair of teetering
stiletto heels and parasol—from tip
to toe in matching lurid pink,
strutting his jet-glow black and
body-built stuff from side to side
in flagrant full gay pride
parading down Fifth Avenue.

From giant urns outside our church
we plied the passers-by with plastic
cups "o' kindness yet" on a hot June
afternoon—"in Jesus' name."
Fully clothed, and more,
dark clergy suit, black shirt and
stiff white collar, I stood my ground,
clutching a tray of cooling draughts
to represent a welcome and a blessing—
at the least—as child of God.

Beaming, he tripped across bestowing
smiles, spectacular, on all and sundry,
chiefly me. Daintily he took the cup
I offered, leaned perilous close—
those tipping heels!—and kissed me on one
startled cheek, his bristles coarse, lips—
generous smile notwithstanding—brushing
deep, appalled revulsion through my gut,

despite all my head was murmuring of
tolerance and Christian love.

"Oh, Reverend," laughed the lady
from the sewing circle,
"you should see the juicy kiss
mark on your cheek." And as we both
dissolved in honest, healing mirth,
first head, then heart took over
from my gut and raised a prayer
of thanks for grace's all-too-often
way of shoving me, still screaming,
toward birth.

. . . for I was hungry and you gave me food,
I was thirsty and you gave me something to drink,
I was a stranger and you welcomed me.
                                    Matt. 25:35 NRSV

Incarnation, when understood in this way, not only
grants permission; it does more than that. It demands that
we seek out and recognize the face of Christ in all of the
manifold and suddenly mysterious encounters that con-
stitute our everyday lives.

Imagination and the Spirit

I have yet many things to say to you,
but you cannot bear them now.
When the Spirit of truth comes,
he will guide you into all the truth. . . .
He will take what is mine and declare it to you.

The doctrine of the Holy Spirit is another fertile source for a theology of the imagination. In the field of international politics, people used to discuss the plight of underdeveloped nations. It seems to me that in theology we have our underdeveloped notions. The *imago Dei* is one, and the Holy Spirit tends to be another, at least in Western thought. We have volumes upon volumes about God the Father, even more concerning God the Son, but precious little still, I would suspect, about God the Holy Spirit. Perhaps this is partly due to the reality that in order to begin to comprehend the Spirit, one must possess the very gift of imagination that only the Spirit bestows.

If one were to judge by typical references to the Holy Spirit in Protestant worship, in prayers, hymns, liturgies, litanies, and the like—yes, and in sermons too—it seems to me that the predominant themes would tend to be those of "Comforter' and "Guide." Now these attributes are all very well and truly, genuinely nice; but the Spirit, at least as described in the Scriptures, is more than that, and at times is not even nice at all. "Comforter" and "Guide" are safe, comfortable and reassuring concepts, but what about the *ruach Yahweh* that rushed upon the judges, leaders, and early prophets of Israel and caused them at times to go berserk? What of the Spirit that descended on the disciples at Pentecost, not as a cozy warm blanket, but as a burning fire; a Spirit that rendered them not so much comforted and guided as blown clean out of their minds?

Indeed the very idea of a *doctrine* of the Spirit seems a contradiction in terms, a true oxymoron. How do you render a flame into a thesis? How does one pin down the wind into a series of dogmatic propositions? After all, "the wind blows where it wills, and you hear the sound of it, but you do not know whence it comes or whither it goes" (John 3:8 RSV).

Certainly in the Scriptures there is an essential link between the Spirit and the workings of the divine imagination. Returning once again to Genesis, the Spirit was involved in the divine action of creation from the very beginning.

> The earth was without form and void,
> and darkness was upon the face of the deep;
> and the Spirit of God was moving over the face of the
> waters.
>
> Gen. 1:2 RSV

And throughout the First Testament the Spirit is seen as that creative power that rushes upon the prophets of Israel and fills them with the inspired Word they are to proclaim (Num. 11:17–29, 1 Sam. 10:6–10, Isa. 11:1–9, Ezek. 8:3, 11:24). This is nowhere more unequivocally stated than in the passage from Isaiah that Jesus selected to read in his home synagogue at Nazareth:

> The spirit of the Lord GOD is upon me,
>   because the LORD has anointed me;
> he has sent me to bring good news to the oppressed,
>   to bind up the brokenhearted,
> to proclaim liberty to the captives,
>   and release to the prisoners;
> to proclaim the year of the LORD's favor.
>
> Isa. 61:1–2 NRSV

In the Second (or New) Testament we are introduced to the concept of a completely new creation, a new creation in Christ, which, as with the "old creation" of Genesis chapter 1, is clearly accomplished by the workings of the Spirit. From the descent of the dove at Christ's baptism through the rebirth by the Spirit described in John (John 3:5–8) to Pentecost itself, at which the gift of the Spirit in tongues of fire signals the inauguration of a whole new covenant community, the Holy Spirit is at its customary task as the expression and the enactment of the divine imagination. And those words "conceived by the Holy Ghost" in the Apostles' Creed recall for us what is the most powerfully imaginative and creative act that has ever been conceived—"conceived" in both the mental and the physical understandings of that word. Another poem by Gerard Manley Hopkins, "God's Grandeur," evokes this same biblical image of the Spirit brooding over the primal chaos, and in doing so communicates more of the reality that is the Holy Spirit than most of the prose-laden works that crowd the shelves of the seminary libraries.

God's Grandeur

The world is charged with the grandeur of God.
> It will flame out, like shining from shook foil;
> It gathers to a greatness, like the ooze of oil
Crushed. Why do men then now not reck his rod?
Generations have trod, have trod, have trod;
> And all is seared with trade; bleared, smeared with
> > toil;
> And wears man's smudge and shares man's smell;
> > the soil
Is bare now, nor can foot feel, being shod.

And for all this, nature is never spent;
    There lives the dearest freshness deep down things;
And though the last lights off the black West went
    Oh, morning, at the brown brink eastward,
        springs—
Because the Holy Ghost over the bent
    World broods with warm breast and with ah! bright
        wings.[26]

I must say that my own experience of the Holy Spirit, such as it has been, has known much more of that "warm breast and . . . ah! bright wings" than it has of those interminable Nicene debates over the *filioque* clause, and whether we dare to affirm that the Spirit actually proceeds from the Son as well as from the Father.

John McIntyre, professor emeritus of divinity at New College, Edinburgh, in a fascinating lecture on theology and imagination delivered during the Edinburgh International Festival of Music and Drama some years ago, argued that it is precisely at Pentecost that we find biblical evidence to support the idea that imagination is, at heart, an essential attribute of God. McIntyre describes Pentecost as

> the expression of the almost uninhibited imagination of God himself, letting himself loose in the lives of men and women and shattering all the complacency not only of the original community, but of the traditionally minded church in every generation. Without blasphemy one could say that the Holy Spirit is the imagination of God let loose in the world.[27]

But then, if the Holy Spirit is God's imagination at work, is it too much to suggest that we in our own imaginations, with the *imago Dei*, that image of God still lurking within us, also know and share, participate in such wild and wonderful workings of the Spirit? Recall again Joan's response to Captain Robert

> [Those voices] come from your imagination. . . . Of course. That is how the message of God comes to us.[28]

Shaw may have been a better theologian than we have given him credit for!

So it is that in our imagination—in the pulpit and elsewhere—we are not just jazzing up our sermons by adding a few frills, scattering a few spices, to enliven a piece of otherwise solid exegesis. I would argue instead, along with Henry Ward Beecher, that imagination is the one absolute essential to the preacher. Without it the sermon is Spiritless in the fullest and most theological sense of that word.

Imagination at its highest is nothing less, I would suggest, than the work of that pentecosting Spirit of God making us intoxicated enough to see and say things that have never been seen or said in precisely that way before. The imagination is that *Ruach Yahweh* flapping its vast wings over the murky chaos of the primeval void and imagining a world for God then to create.

God's Imagining and Ours

> And it shall come to pass afterward,
> 　　that I will pour out my spirit on all flesh;
> your sons and your daughters shall prophesy,
> 　　your old men shall dream dreams,

and your young men shall see visions.
Even upon the menservants and the maidservants
   in those days, I will pour out my spirit.
                              Joel 2:28–29 RSV

All of this, of course—the ongoing creative action of
God, the call to humanity to join God as cocreator, the discerning of the presence of the risen Christ manifest in all
creation, and the work of the brooding Holy Ghost inspiring, and that means *breathing into*, all we do and are the
fire of his or her imagining—requires that we keep our
eyes open, that we stay constantly aware. The motto of
such an approach to preaching might well be, "There is
more to this (far more in fact) than meets the eye." But I
will deal with this at greater length in chapter 4. A poem
by Warren Lane Molton, a friend and former colleague in
campus ministry, captures much of what I have been trying to say about creation, about incarnation, about imagination.

If God Is a Clown
If God is a clown working the crowd
     of this three ring circus
     and letting himself be chased around
     by a toothless old tiger called Satan,
     and, with a single stroke
     of his paper-tassel whip
     and a puff of smoke, he makes Satan
     magically disappear through a trapdoor
     into the crackling hell
     of a sawdust pit;
If God is clowning around with me,

setting me on his knee
and with lollipops and balloons
telling me that all is well,
only to drop me
through that same trapdoor
into a hell of merely dying;
If, indeed, God in Christ is clowning,
setting reality on its ear
with a Gospel hard to hear
that the weak are strong,
the meek inherit the earth,
and with faith in him and new birth
even death means life eternal,
only to let me sleep that great sleep
forever . . .

Well then,
what a circus this has been,
and how I've loved
the lions, tigers and bears,
the dancing elephants and calliope,
even the bazooka band
and the high-wire acts
with all those shining faces looking up;
But, oh that majordomo,
that solitary clown
who loved us children so,
who soothed our fears
and made us laugh with joy to tears
and feel loved . . .
I shall dream of him
forever.[29]

Chapter 3

STEPS TOWARD DELIGHT

❧❧❧❧

The Spirit of the Lord is upon me,
   because he has anointed me
      to bring good news to the poor.
He has sent me to proclaim release to the captives
   and recovery of sight to the blind,
      to let the oppressed go free,
to proclaim the year of the Lord's favor.
                        Luke 4:18 NRSV

Introductory Issues

In this chapter I want to anticipate some of the critical response, and feedback to what has been proposed so far, by offering something utterly down to earth and practical. "After all," fellow preachers might say, "it's all very well for you, a published poet, to do some of these crazy things in your preaching, but I wouldn't even know how to begin to go about it." I offer the following suggestions—"Helpful Hints For Creative Preaching" you might call them—in the spirit of Henry Ward Beecher himself, whose inaugural Beecher Lectures included eminently practical chapters on "Sermon Making," "Health, as Related to Preaching," "Rhetorical Drill and General Training," and "The Study of Human Nature." I do not intend, however, as he did, to recommend phrenology— the comparative study of human skull types—as a particularly useful guide. Although I could not help wondering, as I read that section, how many of the varied homiletical devices now in vogue will seem similarly absurd at the opening of the twenty-second century. But how *does* one "go about it," how does one turn loose, set free the imagination to assume its proper role as the foundation for effective preaching?

And before going any further, it might be helpful to add a word about one of the typical devices I use to launch into a sermon, and that is to open with an amusing story or a joke. I used to indulge in these preliminary tales, not just for the fun of it, but also in an attempt to set the congregation at ease right at the outset. Then I came across a fascinating report in *Scientific American* magazine about optical illusions, specifically those illusions called "reversible figures," in which one sees alternating, and quite contrasting images in the same picture—a white vase between two black faces is one of the most common examples. Brain scientists, studying this phenomenon, have located what appears to be a kind of switch in the brain that shuttles perception back and forth between that organ's left and right hemispheres, and seems to be responsible for these alternating interpretations of one and the same reality. And one of the ways they found to trigger that switch was laughter:

> Among all twenty volunteers tested a good belly laugh either obliterated the . . . phenomenon altogether or

significantly reduced it. . . . Laughter (the researcher speculated) either short circuits the switch or toggles it so fast that we see both interpretations at once. "It resets the brain, or literally creates a new state of mind."

So before you hit them with your daring new ideas or wildly imaginative images, make them laugh, toggle that switch, clear the slate, and thus open them up to alternative interpretations of reality. It helps, of course, to employ that same creative imagination to find a way to relate your introductory story to the more serious stuff that follows. A weekly "opening joke" with no tie-in whatsoever to anything else in the service, can swiftly wear pretty thin.

While on the general subject of method, one further word. My method in these chapters, as in most of my preaching, is less that of logical argument, a carefully reasoned step-by-step presentation of a thesis or viewpoint, the kind of thing one might strive for in a lecture or other academic presentation; more a weaving together of images, poetry, incidents, scenes and vignettes, along with suggestions, testimony, hints from other imaginers. All of which are intended to convey, not so much a well-argued and persuasive conclusion, but rather an experience, an encounter with transcendence, with awe perhaps and mystery, with wonder, surprise, outrage at times and shame, above all, with grace.

Not too long ago, at a library book sale on our summer island in Maine, I picked up Andre Malraux's *Anti Memoirs*, a volume described as "among the most significant

works of this (the twentieth) century." Some of the translation is difficult and dense, a challenge to the persever-
ance of the reader. But then one comes upon luminous
passages like this one:

> Having lived in the shifting realms of intellect and
> imagination all artists share, then in the realms of
> combat and of history . . . I have experienced time and
> again, in humble or dazzling circumstances, those
> moments when the mystery of life appears to each
> one of us as it appears to almost every woman when
> she looks into a child's face and to almost every man
> when he looks into the face of someone dead. In the
> multifarious forms of that which drives us on, in all
> that I have seen of man's struggle against humiliation,
> and even in that sweetness which one can scarcely
> believe exists on this earth, life, like the gods of van-
> ished religions, appears to me at times as if it were the
> libretto for some unknown music.[1]

It is that libretto and its mysterious enigmatic music that
I seek to detect, to disclose, even perhaps to amplify just
a bit, whenever I stand in the pulpit. And I have adopted
that same goal and method in writing this book.

The Essentials

> The Spirit of the Lord is upon me,
>   because he has anointed me
>   to bring good news to the poor.
> He has sent me to proclaim release to the captives
>   and recovery of sight to the blind,
>   to let the oppressed go free,
> to proclaim the year of the Lord's favor.

Now to the actual process of sermon preparation. The first essential requirement is, and must be, time: time set aside from all the pressures and demands of the modern parish—phone calls, faxes, e-mails, and those myriad daily consultations on the urgent minutiae of congregational management and life. I recently heard a speaker describe the modern clergy as "a quivering mass of availability." And that eager and perpetual availability all too often means that there is little or no time left for serious preparation, for the time-demanding, sheer, hard, concentrated slog of the preaching task.

My own discipline in this area resulted from a decisive intervention on the part of my wife, Mhairi, fairly early in my preaching ministry. I was in my first post as a parish minister, after two college chaplaincy positions in which, as host to a series of eminent guest pulpiteers, I had enjoyed the opportunity to preach only once a month. Weekly sermon preparation had just become a new and demanding assignment, and I found myself regularly laboring late into Saturday night to be ready for the next day. With three young children on her hands, this was no fun for Mhairi, and so, after one particularly tedious and exhausting weekend, she issued her ultimatum. "I and the children need you on the weekends. Either you have a sermon ready by Friday suppertime, or there will *be* no Friday suppertime."

I caught the gentle hint, and from then on, except in the most unusual circumstances, I arrived home Friday evening, sometimes a little late to be sure, but relaxed and smiling, with a preachable sermon tucked safely into my briefcase. Of course I usually stole a couple of hours at some point on Saturday, and again early Sunday morning, to look over my material and tighten (or even lighten) it up. But I have been grateful to Mhairi ever since for reminding me of my responsibilities to my calling as husband and father, as well as those as preacher.

Consequently, for me at least, Friday became set aside for sermon writing. After morning staff prayers I would retire to my study, not to be disturbed except in a genuine pastoral emergency, and spend the remainder of the morning reading, note taking and pulling together earlier research, and then the entire afternoon in writing. That particular schedule worked for me; but it will not do so for everyone. The important point is to set time aside, a definite and clearly defined time each week, and then to protect that time jealously for one of the most central responsibilities of your ordination to the ministry of Word and Sacrament. There are, or should be, others in the parish who can make telephone calls, run errands, attend meetings; others, even, who can carry out routine home or hospital calls. Yours is the unique vocation and training, that fits you to climb into that pulpit Sunday morning and preach the gospel. Preach it with everything you've got.

Space is important too: a place apart from your daily office, telephone, intercom, and e-mail, a place of quietness and prayer where, with your books around you, and a minimum of distraction, you can focus on what is, I believe, the most demanding and yet vital task that I have ever known, the bringing of God's Word to life. Of course, such a dedicated study space will not always be readily available. During my sixteen years in Swarthmore, Pennsylvania, for example, I simply lugged the relevant books with me every Friday and claimed a quiet spot in a corner of the church parlor.

I say a place of prayer, and that prayer, needless to say, is also vital. Prayer transforms any space into holy space; or perhaps better said, prayer reveals and recognizes the intrinsic holiness that awaits in each and every place. But it is crucial that such holiness be both perceived and acknowledged. It is crucial that the preparation to proclaim the Word of God be carried out within the milieu of the sacred, and in the context of authentic and persistent prayer. G. K. Chesterton writes thus of his own sense of acknowledging that holiness:

> You say Grace before meals.
> All right.
> But I say grace before the play and opera,
> and grace before the concert
> and pantomime,
> And grace before I open a book,
> And grace before sketching,
> painting,
> Swimming, fencing, boxing, walking, playing, dancing,
> And grace before I dip the pen in the ink.[2]

Today I suspect that most preachers would have to add: "And grace before I boot up the computer!" But however and wherever you choose to prepare, it is essential that your preparation be undergirded by, and sustained within a dialog of, stillness, meditation, and prayer.

> Be still and know that I am God.
>
> Ps. 46:10

After what was said about symbolism in the preceding chapter, it might not be surprising that my own "sermon space" is populated, not only by my books and filing cabinets, but also by a growing collection of objects gathered during various travels and events that speak to me of the holy, which evoke in me a fuller awareness of the sacred dimensions of my days. As I reflect upon my chosen text, my eyes wander across a strangely dark Madonna and Child from Czestochowa in Poland, a stained-glass cross from Hawaii, a communion token from Scotland, a piece of kente cloth from Ghana, and a battered remnant from a German incendiary bomb that fell outside my boyhood home one clamorous, siren-filled night in 1941. These are all mementos, in the deepest sense of that word; they help me to remember where I have been, what I have seen, and who I have become as a result of all this. And so, as with the Deuteronomist theologian of the Hebrew Scriptures, having retraced the hand of God in what has been, and being renewed in trust for the present moment, I can regard whatever lies ahead with that faith that is the foundation for all authentic preaching of the Word.

The Place of Time

> The Spirit of the Lord is upon me,
> because he has anointed me
> to bring good news to the poor.

He has sent me to proclaim release to the captives
    and recovery of sight to the blind,
      to let the oppressed go free,
to proclaim the year of the Lord's favor.

I began by stressing the importance of time—of setting aside a specific time, and in this context of prayer I would add that there must be sufficient of it. Time, in other words, for more than simply cramming over the commentaries or the canned pablum (for the most part) on the Internet. Time for genuine reflection; and reflection means looking deep into the stillness, and discovering yourself, and the world which surrounds you, portrayed and illuminated there. It seems to me—and even more so as I get older—that it is only in reflection that we can come anywhere close to figuring out what is really going on. In the heat of the action we simply do what has to be done. Most of the time, to be completely honest, we are in survival mode. It is only later, looking back, that we begin to realize everything that was actually involved.

I am convinced that the Scriptures were largely written in that fashion—retrospectively, looking back over the shoulder, as it were. When the Red Sea opened up, don't you suspect that Moses had little time to meditate upon God or divine providence right then?

Let's get these people out of here! Move it, now, before the Egyptians see it too.

But then later, looking back:

So that's what was going on So that's what Yahweh had in mind, that's what our God was up to all along.

And isn't that also true of our own lives, and of our sermon preparation? We need time, time and solitude, to wrestle with the text, to wrestle with today, to try out all kinds of crazy, or at least improbable, ideas, who knows what will emerge from them (Write them down, write them down! As Ernest Campbell used to say of all such ideas, "It's better to have them and not need them, than need them and not have them"), and then to sift through all of this, separating wheat from chaff, setting some ideas aside for another week, another sermon, and gradually, and prayerfully, focusing in on what it is the Lord has for us to say right there, right then.

This kind of exploration led me to a poem some months ago. I called it Recollection":

I have a hunch that much of faith
is formed in looking backward,
taking stock, reflecting on
what has been, and what might have been.
Most of the time, you see,
we're far too close to things
to view them properly.
The hassle hustle of the everyday
can blind us to what's really going on,
obscure for us the chasms and the pinnacles
that mark the landscape of our living.
It's only when, and if, we take the time
to glance across the shoulder and reflect,
to pause and ponder where we are
and how we got here, that we can trace
the constant presence of a mystery
that blesses as it wounds,
that turns us inside out and upside down,

that leads us, by a path we did not choose,
toward a hope we hardly knew we had,
a trust that yet endures, despite so much,
a strange familiar grace that touches
everything we touch with promise.
I'll even bet old stammering Moses
leading his motley crew across that gap
between the waves, had no time to inquire about
who put it there. He just saw a chance
and grabbed it with both hands. Then later,
on the other bank, or deep into the wilderness,
he realized, "So that's what God
was up to all the time!"[3]

Part of this precious time set apart, an essential part, must be for wasting time; for what Robert Dykstra, in his book *Discovering a Sermon*, describes as "uncensored daydreaming."[4] Brenda Ueland in her delightfully quirky little book *If You Want to Write* dubs this part of the process "moodling":

> So you see the imagination needs moodling—long, inefficient, happy idling, dawdling and puttering. These people who are always briskly doing something and as busy as waltzing mice, they have little, sharp, staccato ideas, such as: "I see where I can make an annual cut of $3.47 in my meat budget." But they have no slow, big ideas. And the fewer consoling, noble, shining, free, jovial, magnanimous ideas that come, the more nervously and desperately they rush and run from office to office and up and downstairs, thinking by action at last to make life have some warmth and meaning.[5]

I cannot begin to count the number of times I have moodled, set a sermon aside, often in midstream, and taken a walk through the church gardens, or around the city block, even caught a brief nap on the study sofa; in other words, I have let my mind lie fallow, and then returned to the task with inspiration renewed. Despite all of today's mounting pressures to do otherwise, we must devote time, major blocks of time, to our preaching.

On the other hand, it is also possible to spend too much time in this manner, or to spend that time unwisely. In the preparation of every sermon there comes what I call "the fish-or-cut-bait moment," the moment at which you have to set aside the books, the reflections too, and commence putting words on paper, or onto a computer screen. It can be seductive, even most enjoyable, to continue to pursue research or to tease out ideas and possibilities at ever greater length. But Sunday morning looms— or in my case, Friday suppertime—and ideas in your head, however entrancing, are not going to be transferred into those heads in the pews until they are set down, connected, and brought to a conclusion by means of the most powerful and effective words and phrases you can find. And that is sheer hard work, and so most of us, I suspect, have a tendency to put it off for as long as possible.

Suspicion and Courage

> The Spirit of the Lord is upon me,
>   because he has anointed me
>   to bring good news to the poor.
> He has sent me to proclaim release to the captives
>   and recovery of sight to the blind,

to let the oppressed go free,
to proclaim the year of the Lord's favor.

Linked to everything mentioned so far is a quality of
deep suspicion—you could even call it an insistent opti-
mism—a suspicion that things actually do hang together,
that the story you read last night, that news item on TV this
morning, the concert you recently attended, the movie
you saw, the joke you overheard, the panhandler who
approached you in the subway, and yes, this ancient text in
the Scriptures, may be connected somehow; and what fun
it might be to figure it out. The more I read these Scriptures,
and I'm sure I am not alone in this discovery, the more
dimensions of meaning, sometimes wild and wonderful
meaning, I uncover within these old, familiar words. We
need to approach these Scriptures with an attitude of
expectancy and openness, available and ready for the Spirit
to reveal to us, and through us to our people, the deep inter-
connectedness of things, that same sense of overarching
providence that sustained our forebears in the faith.

Then there is courage—not the heroic stuff of dramatic events and disasters, but the sheer week-by-week
guts to try something different, something that may leave
you flat on your face in front of a good many onlookers.
The two scariest moments for a preacher are said to be
when the congregation are not paying attention . . . and
when they are! It does take courage to preach, if you are
really preaching. Faith, after all, is about taking risks,
gambling, even betting your life. How then can we
attempt to preach this faith in a timorous way? How can

one proclaim "release to the captives" while clinging to the homiletical life preservers?

In this matter of boldness, I well recall a young woman minister—Mary Speers—preaching her first ever sermon in the lofty, balcony-level, Harry Emerson Fosdick pulpit, at First Presbyterian in New York City. She climbed the steep stone steps, took a firm grip on the elegant carved oak, gazed out and down across the expectant congregation, and said:

> Do you remember at the pool, the first time you scrambled all the way up the ladder to the top of the high dive, and when you got up there, and walked out to the end, and then looked down . . . all you just wanted was to climb back down again . . .

As an introduction, for a young, novice preacher, in an intimidating setting, the picture she painted was brilliant. Yet it struck me at the time that there is also a sense, an important, even vital sense, in which every preacher should share that semipanic, that moment of profound self-examination, that clutch of giddy vertigo, whenever she or he climbs into a pulpit and pronounces that ancient and prophetic prologue: "Hear the Word of the Lord."

Ernest Campbell, formerly preacher to Riverside Church, once disclosed to me how he evaluates preachers by comparing them with Olympic high-divers. In those gold-medal competitions the contenders are judged, not merely on the way they actually perform their dive, but on the "degree of difficulty" of the dive they elect to attempt. Judged on a similar basis, Campbell remarked, most of us preachers would fail miserably, because we tend to tackle the easiest of questions, the most dried-out and tindery of straw men, the most tired and worked over of issues, or we content ourselves with telling and retelling that old, old, extremely old story, in the same old way it has been told from the very beginning.

In order to succeed, you have to have the courage to risk failure, and there will be times when your efforts do seem to fall on stony ground. But that is hardly a new experience for preachers of the gospel, or for many of us. And when and as it works for you, when and as the Spirit recognizes its own unique flame kindling within your words, and then kindles that same spark in the souls of your people, then you have come to what the Shaker hymn writer calls "the valley of love and delight."

The Need for Trust

The Spirit of the Lord is upon me,
    because he has anointed me
        to bring good news to the poor.
He has sent me to proclaim release to the captives
    and recovery of sight to the blind,
        to let the oppressed go free,
to proclaim the year of the Lord's favor.

One resource for this necessary courage should be a renewed sense of trust about the task you are engaged in. Trust in the Lord and God's bold, wild, inspiring Spirit, who surely will not permit the Word to be sown in vain but, right there alongside the barren and stony ground, provides fertile rich soil that will bring forth "some an hundredfold, some sixtyfold, some thirtyfold." (Matt. 13:18 KJV). Trust in your call, that the Lord has had a purpose for you all along, and will use you for it, no matter what you do or do not do, say or do not say. Trust also, and faith too, in your congregation, that they are not totally dense and can be trusted to pick up, for example, references and even subtle allusions without your having to hammer them home in crude, blatantly obvious and almost patronizing ways. That cynical old business they used to teach in seminary:

> Tell them what you're going to tell them.
> Tell them what you have to tell them.
> Then tell them what you have told them.

How utterly boring! And how arrogantly patronizing! That kind of preaching, like a self-fulfilling prophecy, will attract only the most unimaginative and lifeless of listeners. Ernest Campbell has remarked that every congregation has two types of listeners, the poetic and the prudential. Since the prudential types get to hear what they like for 167 hours of every week, surely there ought to be at least one hour somewhere for the poetic.

I cherish the memory of a poetry reading one Sunday in a small midwestern college town. I had preached for the college baccalaureate service in the morning, and the local Presbyterian congregation piggybacked on that event to invite me to read there in the evening. When I got to the church, the hall was more-than-half-filled with the usual enthusiastic gaggle of literary ladies, but they were accompanied by their husbands, their midwestern farmer husbands, with rugged, red, weather-beaten faces, enormous calloused hands, and all squeezed into their Sunday best suits, looking thoroughly out of place and miserable. What could these men possibly get from a poetry reading? I asked myself, as I chatted with some of them during the inevitable preliminary potluck supper. Still, I took courage and launched out upon the deep. And to my amazement, their comments, their questions and suggestions pointed out things in the poems—*my* poems!—that I hadn't even realized were in there. They were listening to, and hearing, the poems from a quite different perspective than I had used as the author; and their contributions were for the most part pertinent, helpful, and, on occasion, profound.

I am convinced—and on the basis of rich experience too—that given half a chance, granted just a smidgen of encouragement and nurture, the creative imagination that lies within all of us (that *imago Dei* again) will spring to vibrant and creative life. And that if we preachers neglect to foster this gift in our people, in this most prosaic of times, we are failing them miserably. "Most hockey players skate to where the puck is." Said the great Gretsky in an interview: "I skate to where it's going to be." Try that in your preaching. Quit patronizing the saints of God. Start giving your people something to stretch for, to grow into, to skate toward.

Stories

> The Spirit of the Lord is upon me,
>   because he has anointed me
>   to bring good news to the poor.

> He has sent me to proclaim release to the captives
> and recovery of sight to the blind,
> to let the oppressed go free,
> to proclaim the year of the Lord's favor.

Add to all of the above an abiding love for words and stories. Ernest Somerville again, who taught me so much of the craft of preaching, used to say:

"In all my years of preaching, in this country and abroad, no one has ever come to me and said, 'Dr. Somerville, I have never forgotten that brilliant third point you made on the doctrine of the atonement when you preached here years ago.' But I cannot count the number of people who come to me and say, 'Dr. Somerville, I will never forget that story you told about . . .'"

There is something about a story, something about an eternal truth that is embedded, enfleshed—yes, incarnate—within the hopes and fears, joys and tears, fights and feasts and frailties that make up the fabric of our days, something that speaks to us human creatures on a richer, fuller level than any abstract or theoretical presentation of ideas or ideals. Be ever on the lookout for good stories, all kinds of stories—stories in books, plays and movies, newspapers, and over the Internet too. And when you find one, treasure it, copy it down, because even if not this week or this month, its time will come, and it will serve you, your preaching, and the gospel well.

This quest for stories leads quite naturally to the subject of reading matter, of grist for the homiletical mill. There are those—especially persons in temporal, spatial, or intellectual proximity to a theological seminary—who would restrict the pastoral library to theology, ethics, biblical studies, and closely related materials. I cannot imagine a more effective way to drive any potential of "delight" out of the pulpit. Of course, such reading should form a regular portion of the preacher's diet, but my own tastes lean heavily toward the omnivorous. Newspapers, magazines, biography, novels, plays, movies, and poetry all provide valuable resources to the individual who is obliged to come up with something fresh and relevant at least once a week. It was William Carlos Williams who wrote:

> It is difficult
> to get the news from poems
> Yet men die miserably every day
> For lack
> Of what is found there.[6]

I have found it important to pay attention to areas in which my own background is relatively weak. Too much of what we read, particularly as we grow older, tends to be material we already know and completely agree with. In my own case, as one who had major difficulties in school in the areas of mathematics and science, I make a point of keeping up with *Scientific American*. Now I admit I don't really understand all, or even most, of what I read there, but I am also surprised at how much I can figure out. In the pages of that magazine, and of the Tuesday Science section of the *New York Times*, I am regularly astonished, even mind-boggled, by the sheer achievement of today's scientific community. From the infinitely tiny world of the quantum to the furthest reaches of the universe, and

77

even other universes yet to be explored, the human brain, and its brilliant technology, have achieved miracles in our time in exploring and explaining the workings and the grandeur of God's cosmic creation. And these insights too must find their place within the preaching of our time, or we risk being relegated once again to the Dark Ages.

Words for The Word

> The Spirit of the Lord is upon me,
>> because he has anointed me
>>> to bring good news to the poor.
> He has sent me to proclaim release to the captives
>> and recovery of sight to the blind,
>>> to let the oppressed go free,
> to proclaim the year of the Lord's favor.

As for words—these are the working tools of our trade. Treat them with care. Value them for their specificity; there's usually a wrong word and a right, or a least a better word. Treasure them for their variety. There is almost always more than one good way to say a thing. Mix the words up a bit, like a baseball pitcher. After all, one fastball after another can be, if nothing else, intimidating. And deploy your words with a strict and severe economy. In my own experience as both preacher and writer, all first drafts are insufferably verbose, and I suspect I am not alone in this tendency. One of the weekly exercises we were set in theology class at Edinburgh University was to reduce one hundred pages of Karl Barth to ten. It seemed

needlessly tedious at the time, but it taught me clear thinking and concise writing. Like a sculptor with a raw block
of marble, we need to carve and chip away at our material
until only what is absolutely necessary remains. Time
spent thus in crafting a sermon reaps untold dividends in
clarity and overall impact. Wordiness and windiness are
two of the greatest threats to effective preaching, and to
even the faintest possibility of delight.

Give words your ear too. Remember that, although
you may be writing them down, or typing them on a
screen somewhere, they are not going to be seen or read
at all; they are going to be heard. So listen to your sermons; "lend them your ears"; pay attention to rhythm,
rhyme, and euphony, to harmony and discord, alliThera-
tion, onomatopoeia, and the like. In a review of a Carnegie
Hall recital by the Welsh baritone Bryn Terfel, Paul Griffiths of the *New York Times* wrote a hymn to words and
their proper employment that spills over from the concert
hall and sets standards also for the pulpit:

> Mr. Terfel loves words, loves the sounds of words,
> and loves giving them to his audience in huge
> bunches of variegated colors. He can roar—with pain,
> with pleasure, with fierce indignation, filling the hall
> with full strong tone. But he can also coo and purr at
> an extreme pianissimo, making a sound that stays
> audible only because there is so much in it to feel, as
> well as to hear.
>
> This is crucial. Words, clearly, are not what Mr.
> Terfel's artistry is all about; he is a great storyteller,
> and wonderful words, wonderful sounds, are his
> means to make his stories live.[7]

I would venture to suggest that we preachers have a great deal to learn from the way an artist like Bryn Terfel can hold an audience spellbound.

In sharp contrast with the way an artist like Terfel prepares, however, the actual delivery of the sermon tends nowadays to be the orphaned child of the preacher's preparation. The great singer, of course, is quite consciously and deliberately preparing for a performance. Most homileticians would be extremely reluctant to describe anything they do in the pulpit as a "performance," assuming that such an approach implies "mere" playacting, and thus insincerity. Yet I have seen many otherwise excellent sermons rendered almost completely ineffectual because of thoughtless and inept delivery. With our heavy seminary emphasis on the academic side of things, we tend to put all our effort into content, into what we are going to say, and spend little or no time on how we plan to say it.

Listening to your sermons involves speaking them aloud, hearing them just as the congregation will hear them, paying close attention to possible confusions due to emphasis, accent, or pronunciation. On the matter of accents there are those—especially among folk of the Presbyterian persuasion—who maintain that a Scots accent can offer a genuine advantage. I have even heard it said that

> A burr in the pulpit
> is worth a thousand on the paycheck.

Unfortunately, no one ever told that to any of the kirk sessions I worked with. Dr. Somerville, whose mellow, west-of-Scotland accent charmed not only those in the pews but thousands over the radio, used to tell of folk asking him why he invariably spent his summer vacations back in Scotland. He would reply, "Round about June every year, my congregation starts to understand what I'm saying, so I have to go back home to brush up my accent." Polish your words, then, and craft them, so that they can not only reach the listening ears, but unseal and open them, charm them, tug on them just a bit, lead them on and in, to where the way, the truth, the life can be revealed.

Gaps

The Spirit of the Lord is upon me,
    because he has anointed me
        to bring good news to the poor.
He has sent me to proclaim release to the captives
    and recovery of sight to the blind,
        to let the oppressed go free,
to proclaim the year of the Lord's favor.

In this regard too, be sure to leave plenty of room for the Spirit to work. I mean by this to emphasize the importance of providing gaps, empty spaces—creative distances, if you like—those moments in your preaching when the spark can leap across and make its own vital connections, connections that may set off a chain of thought you could never have predicted; there's trust involved here too. Some years ago I delivered a lecture in the William Belden Noble series at Harvard University under the title "The God of the Gaps Revisited." Part of my

81

thesis was that Bishop Robinson's historic rejection of "the God of the gaps," spelled out in his 1960s bestseller *Honest to God*, needed to be revisited. I have found some of the most fertile areas for imaginative insight and creativity occurring precisely in those "gap" areas, those moments when things simply do not add up, those occasions when the times seem distinctly out of joint, those debates that end in deadlock and a seemingly inevitable paradox. Robert Dykstra, again, quotes journalist Ann Fadiman:

> I have always felt that the action most worth watching is not at the center of things but where the edges meet. I like shorelines, weather fronts, international borders. There are interesting frictions and incongruities in these places, and often, if you stand at the point of tangency, you can see both sides better than if you were in the middle of either one.[8]

Summers, when I go fishing in Maine's Casco Bay, I often take my boat into the choppiest, most turbulent water, where currents meet, reefs rise sharply close to the surface, or deep channels draw together. The fishing is usually excellent there, where the water is particularly alive, stirred up and full of oxygen and rich food. Hugh MacDiarmid, this past century's most acclaimed Scots poet, in his epic *A Drunk Man Looks at the Thistle*, writes:

> I'll hae nae hauf-way hoose, but aye be whaur
> Extremes meet—it's the only way I ken
> To dodge the curst conceit o' bein' richt
> That damns the vast majority o' men.[9]

Or, in English:

I'll have no halfway house, but always be where
extremes meet—it's the only way I know
to dodge the cursed conceit of being right
that damns the vast majority of us.

And it's that "curst conceit o' bein' richt" that is tearing so much apart in both society and church right now.

If only we preachers didn't have to be right all the time. If only we could do as Jesus did and answer questions with further questions, not with indisputably correct answers. If only we could take our stance astride some of those gaps in our society, the intellectual distances, as one artist in my Greenwich Village congregation described them to me, areas of dispute and controversy too, and then exercise our creative imaginations in that most fertile setting to discern what God is up to, to ask the questions Christ is still posing to us, questions to which there may well be no correct answers as yet.

Indeed you'd think our pastoral counseling experience would teach us that it's not really about giving answers at all. It's about being there—being there and truly paying attention. And then, from time to time, just asking the right questions. My poem "Secret" expresses this same thought in a different way:

Secret
The truth, or so he came
to tell us, will not be caught
and held within the ordered paragraphs
and pages of a treatise or elaborated dogma,
does not lend itself to concise delineation

or precise and tidily presented definition,
is never to be found locked tight inside
those capsulated catch-word phrases,
slogans, live-or-die-for credos that we love
to force down one another's throats.
Rather is to be glimpsed across a table,
fireside, subway car, or early morning meadow,
a late lingering fragrance, echo of tears
or laughter, a child's response to
this world's daily mystery, a gift revealed
in every moment we can look and listen
to each other, see, and sing that living truth
that woos us, weds us, weaves us in
and through the holy fabric of our days.

Sermons without gaps in them, sermons with no "nothing" there, no intellectual distances, sermons that arrive gift-wrapped, with all loose ends neatly tied in doctrinal red ribbon, can also be sermons that leave no room for the Spirit to work in. They leave no room for that creative spark—*imago Dei*—within the hearers to spring toward new life. How marvelous to have people leave the sanctuary scratching their heads now and then, saying, "I'm not sure just what she was getting at there," and then discussing it, even arguing about it, over Sunday lunch, and chewing it over for the next several days!

I have never forgotten James Dittes's basic pastoral counseling course as I experienced it at Yale. Instead of a lot of technical reading in psychology, psychiatry, and the like, he assigned novels: *One Day in the Life of Ivan Denisovich*, *I Never Promised You a Rose Garden*, and one almost soft-porn paperback—I seem to have repressed the title—

about a young whore who was called, as I recall, "Pussy." He didn't explain, or justify his choices either, just said, more or less, "Go figure"—not unlike Jesus with his parables, in fact. Maybe we should end all our sermons that way: not with an "Amen"—or as one Presbyterian colleague in Manhattan does, "The Word of the Lord!"—but with, "Go figure!"

So much, then, for sermon preparation. I'm afraid that, for many of us at least, it is all a bit like the proverbial verdict on sausage making: "If you knew what went into it, you'd be a lot less interested in what came out of it." However, we must never lose sight of the ultimate goal of these rather mundane considerations. Frederick Buechner, in his early novel *The Final Beast*, records a conversation between two friends, Nicolet and Denbigh, about reality and faith:

> "If the life of faith was a dance, Denbigh, and this was the only music—all you could hear anyway—" with a few more double raps he began to suggest a kind of erratic rhythm"—do you think a man could dance it, Denbigh?"
>
> "It sounds like calypso or something. I suppose you could dance to it," Denbigh said. "I'm not sure what you're talking about."
>
> "I'm not sure what I'm talking about either." He tossed the rung toward the barn which it struck and fell. "But whatever this is we move around through . . ." He raked his hand slowly back and forth through the air. "Reality . . . the air we breathe . . . this emptiness . . . If you could get hold of it by the corner somewhere, just slip your fingernail underneath and peel it back enough to find what's there behind it, I think you'd be

> . . . I think the dance that must go on back there," Nicolet began, "way down deep at the heart of space, where being comes from . . . There's dancing there, Denbigh. My kids have dreamed it. Emptiness is dancing there. The angels are dancing. And their feet scatter new worlds like dust . . . If we saw any more of that dance than we do, it would kill us sure," Nicolet said. "The glory of it."[10]

"If you could get hold of it (reality) by the corner somewhere, just slip your fingernail underneath and peel it back enough to find what's there behind it . . ." That's what we are about, finally. Disclosing the dance. Unveiling the deepest dimensions of reality. Discovering and then revealing grace; the presence and the power, at times even the purpose, of the Almighty One—the creator and redeemer—who awaits us in this garden of creation. And we mistake the creator for the gardener. But that quest will form the topic of my final chapter.

Chapter 4

LOOKING FOR THE RESURRECTION

⁂

Now faith is the assurance of things hoped for,
the conviction of things not seen.
                                        Heb. 11:1 NRSV

God's Spies

In one of Frederick Buechner's continuing meditative dia-
logues with *King Lear*, he reminds us of that terrible/won-
derful scene near the end as Lear and Cordelia, finally
reconciled, are led away to prison—and, as it turns out, to
death. Shakespeare gives us these words from the aged
king:

> . . . Come, let's away to prison:
> we two alone will sing like birds i' the cage: . . .
> And take upon 's the mystery of things,
> As if we were God's spies.
>   Act V, Scene 3[1]

What if that was what poets, and imaginative preachers too, were really up to? What if we were called to be
God's spies—to be those, in other words, who notice

87

things, who truly pay attention, and who bring back regular reports on what they have seen, what they believe is actually afoot?

The true task of revelation, after all, the role of prophecy as we encounter it in the Bible, is not so much to foretell the future—or so the biblical scholars tell us—as it is to perceive and report back on what is really happening here and now. The longer I share this most challenging vocation, to bring God's word to life, the longer I experience this mysterious working of the Spirit—blowing where it listeth—the more I see our calling in this light, to

> ... take upon 's the mystery of things,
> as if we were God's spies,

or as Saint Paul puts it, to be "stewards of the mysteries of God" (1 Cor. 4:1 RSV), to be those who, in the service of this heavenly espionage, train themselves to perceive the hidden realities of existence, those truths that lie just beneath the surface of everyday phenomena and events but are routinely ignored in the hectic pace of the daily round.

What, then, might we be spying for? For what sorts of things must we be on the alert? In my daily devotions I use a little book I bought while a student in seminary, John Doberstein's *Minister's Prayer Book.*[2] My copy is, at this stage, pretty tattered and torn; but I know it now and, over the years, it seems to have come to know me. As part of these spiritual exercises I find myself once a week reciting the Nicene Creed—I'd have it memorized, if they'd only stop changing and updating the words on me. Anyway, just a few months ago I was brought up short by that phrase right near the end—the penultimate clause, in fact—of the entire Nicene Creed: "and I look for the resurrection of the dead."

I've been reciting these ancient words for at least forty years and had always assumed they referred to the far end of time—like that treasure hunt text I cited at the beginning of chapter 1. But on that particular day it struck me, dawned on me for the very first time; maybe I'm supposed to be doing this now—I mean looking for the resurrection of the dead. Might it just be that these timeworn words of hope entail more than expecting something good at the very end, that they call on us, in fact, to begin looking for that resurrection now, this very day, and every day *until* that end of time, whatever it might be, does finally arrive?

> . . . and I look for the resurrection of the dead,
> and the life of the world to come.

Have you glimpsed it lately?

Here is E. B. White, describing, demonstrating, intimately living out that clause about looking "for the resurrection of the dead," as he observes Katherine, his wife, during the closing months of her life, planning and planting her garden:

> There she would sit, hour after hour, in the wind and the weather, while Henry Allen produced dozens of brown paper packages of new bulbs and a basketful of old ones, ready for the intricate interment. . . . there was something comical yet touching in her bedraggled

appearance . . . the small hunched-over figure, her studied absorption in the implausible notion that there would be yet another spring, oblivious to the ending of her own days, which she knew perfectly well was near at hand, sitting there with her detailed chart under those dark skies in the dying October, calmly plotting the resurrection.[3]

I wonder if this calm plotting of the resurrection might just be another of the tasks assigned to those who are God's spies.

Signs of Resurrection

Now faith is the assurance of things hoped for, the conviction of things not seen.

I saw a sign of resurrection several years ago at Swarthmore in our church's new memorial garden. The garden is divided into two distinct sections. The area right by the entrance is simply a church garden with manicured lawns, flagstone pathways, weathered benches here and there for quiet relaxation, and a huge old sycamore tree providing shade for the lemonade and cookies served on May-June Sunday mornings after church. Then, through a gap in the ornamental yew hedge, there opens out the actual memorial space, where ashes are interred among the trees and shrubs, and names and dates are inscribed upon bronze plates set in a semicircular chest-high wall of rough and golden Pennsylvania stone. One hot almost-summer Sunday the children from child care had erupted through into

the memorial garden section and were climbing . . . but the
poem will tell the rest.

Un-dividing Wall

It curves in rugged Pennsylvania stone
a cusp, new moon, above the grassy circle
at the center of the church Memorial Garden
a wall dividing life from solid, stony death.
Five feet tall of it, with flagstone brim
and seven plates of bronze to wear
the names and dates which represent
too much for any wall to bear.

Today's picnic for the Sunday school
has spilled across the lawns into this space
preserved for memories and ashes—dust to dust.
Huddled in sycamore shade and sipping punch,
parents watch with mixed response—some anxious,
others smiling, some seem shocked—as eight
and nine and ten-year-olds—defying death—
struggle to scramble up its rough-hewn face,
dance a moment of delight along the parapet,
then dare to leap down to the green below
as if some year-worn craggy granddaddy
had beckoned them to his lap and sat there chuckling
at their wriggling pranks, their shrieks
and whoops and giggles of pure joy.

Walls are for climbing too,
I realized, and launching off the top
into tomorrow seeking flight
from memory into hope,
then landing with a thud where tears are swept away
by peals of lively ever-youthful laughter.[4]

Isaiah it was—Israel's greatest prophet in my book—
who told us that a little child shall lead us. I suspect
that prophecy was not restricted totally to the town of
Bethlehem.

Or did I perhaps spot the resurrection years before in
Wooster, Ohio, while weeding the front lawn one sunny
Easter Sunday afternoon; and then describe it in my poem
"Hope Weed"?

Hope Weed

Our Christian symbols seem, at times, not quite
appropriate to the meaning that they bear.
For instance, take the Easter lily, white
and fragile sign of resurrection. Rare,
its graceful silent trumpet greets the light
of March or April only under glare
of florists' lamps, unnaturally bright.
You never find them in the open air
before July. A better flower for Easter Day
would be, as every angry gardener knows,
the dandelion, seeded by the gay
abandoned wind that, as it listeth, blows.
No matter how we weed out every stray,
digging as deep, the root still deeper goes.
And when, at last, we quit and go away
the rain falls, and a host of fresh bright foes
stands resurrected, and the garden glows.[5]

A favorite moment—dare I call it a vision?—in this
search for the resurrection occurred during a winter vaca-
tion/preaching gig in the U.S. Virgin Islands some years
ago. Here's how I described it and developed it too, in my
Easter sermon a couple of months later.

I saw a resurrection just last February in Saint Thomas. One of the stray dogs that hung around the house we stayed in had caught one of the wild chickens that roosted in the trees. It toyed with it for a while, munched, chomped and nuzzled at it, then left it lying in the driveway. I assumed the poor beast had expired, until it began to give out a series of long, low moans, to which its family in the trees responded with all sorts of squawks and shrieks and cackles. When the bird finally was still, the gardener and I walked over to check things out. The rooster lay there, head in the dust, legs in the air, most obviously dead; but there was no blood, no broken bones, no entrails, only a few loose feathers blowing around. My companion bent down to pick it up but, as soon as he touched one claw, the bird was on its feet, in the air, and flying squawking down the road and up into the nearest tree. The whole thing had been some kind of a game. Maybe they put this on for the tourists! So much of the time we lie in the driveway moaning—don't we? Acting like we're dead, looking like we're dead, feeling like we're dead. And with no thought at all for forever. What if all it took was the gardener's touch to get us on our feet and flying? What if all it took was a moment just like this one to lift our eyes, raise our sights, wing us on our way toward eternity.

Paying Attention

Now faith is the assurance of things hoped for,
the conviction of things not seen.

On the most basic level it's all about paying attention. W. H. Auden somewhere called for what he described as an "intensity of attention," which he claimed forms the essential foundation not just for artistic vision, but for scientific discovery as well. We learn this too from Robert Frost, whose poetry provides a rich source of insight gained from the careful observation of the everyday—and by "careful" here Frost means both heedful and loving, full of care. Frost saw his role, and that of the poet in general, to be that which I have been advocating for the preacher: that of the seer, the one who notices, whose eyes are held wide open, who expects to be surprised, astonished even—I love that line in the Psalter where the psalmist sings of "the wine of astonishment" (Ps. 60:3 KJV)—by the sheer mystery and splendor of the universe. In his poem "The Star Splitter," Frost tells of one Brad McLaughlin, who, as Frost puts it,

> . . . having failed at hugger-mugger farming,
> He burned his house down for the fire insurance
> And spent the proceeds on a telescope
> To satisfy a life-long curiosity
> About our place among the infinities.

When the storyteller inquires of McLaughlin why he did this, he gives the following answer:

> The best thing that we're put here for's to see;
> The strongest thing that's given to us to see with's
> A telescope. Someone in every town
> Seems to me owes it to the town to keep one.
> In Littleton it may as well be me.[6]

How many pastors' studies, I wonder, include a telescope among the working tools, and not necessarily for gazing at the stars, but to further our research about "our place among the infinities"?

John McIntyre, in the Edinburgh Festival lectures I referred to in chapter 2, sees this patient and continual "paying attention" as the basic work of the imagination, indeed, as the action of the Holy Spirit within us. McIntyre challenges us, by means of the imagination.

> perpetually to be on the qui vive (on the alert), so that you may look on the world not just as a thing of sense and appetite, but as the creation of God . . . to develop an attitude of expectancy, a willingness to see what others are not sufficiently perceptive to notice.

Others have called this a readiness to notice and point to the significance of the insignificant, to the presence of the extraordinary within the ordinary. A student of mine a couple of years ago summed this up perfectly when he observed that in our sermon preparation we are usually "too busy looking to see." In the following poem I have tried to call attention to this Spirit-filled dimension of reality.

Significant

You literally make a sign—
at least that's what your Latin signifies—
pick up a magic marker and insert,
inscribe yourself below the cheerful face,
"Hello, my name is . . ."
tack or staple a blank piece of cardboard
right across a slat of lumber scrap
and scrawl upon it what it is you have to say,
whatever it is you love, or hate, or even live for.

"Notice Me!" you call out,
"Pay Attention—Over Here!"
But now supposing, for a moment,
that every single thing might be significant,
and all creation, like those malling throngs
in Washington D.C. massed there
before Abe Lincoln's chair,
is demonstrating, for God's sake, and ours too,
is waving, hailing, placarding to us,
and giving notice, "Here I am now. Heads Up.
Over Here. Stop, Look, and Listen."
There just may be more to this—
don't you see?—than meets the eye.

One of the blessings of my retirement years has been
the opportunity to spend three to four months each year
in an island log cabin perched on a bluff overlooking
Maine's magnificent Casco Bay. Some late September
afternoon I will take a break from closing the place up for
the winter and walk through the long, rustling, waist-
high grasses out toward the point, the East End where we
live. When I finally reach the rocks by the shore, I will
notice that my corduroys or blue jeans are covered with
all kinds of stuff left clinging to them from my brushing
through the undergrowth. I start to brush it off, then stop
a moment, take one tiny piece of whatever it is between
finger and thumb, and break it open. And there it is, life,
seeds, next spring and summer's living green, for these
are seedpods hitching a ride to fertile ground, wherever
that might be.

We preachers need to take another look at the stuff,
the dross, the litter, the tiny, seeming nuisance stuff that

clings and clutters up our days. Just like that common, ordinary loaf of bread, we need to break it open, crack the crust, and find there at its heart, life, the seeds, the promise and the hope that in the very best, and not just the worst sense, what goes around comes around, that every ending is also a beginning, and that

> eye hath not seen, nor ear heard,
> neither have entered into the heart of humankind,
> the things which God hath prepared for them that love
> God.

It's All a Frame-Up

> Now faith is the assurance of things hoped for,
> the conviction of things not seen.

Another way of looking at this treasure hunt, this paying-strict-attention approach to the preacher's task, is to see it all as one gigantic frame-up. One of the highlights of the season on the island in Maine where we spend our summers is the ladies aid fair, a gala occasion at which—apart from the best lobster and crab rolls you ever tasted—you can purchase all kinds of knitted and crocheted items, baked goods, homemade preserves, and a white elephant department that is reputed to conceal untold splendor beneath a surface of apparent kitsch—yet another kind of treasure hunt! This year one of the veteran ladies aid members, a considerable artist, was selling pictures. Some were her own pastels and watercolors, others were photo reproductions of her Hungarian father's dramatic oil paintings of seascapes. These were all available at a ridiculously low price, and nobody seemed to be buying. Mhairi and I, as homegrown Scots ever ready for a bargain, but also as folk who have an eye for interesting art after our years in Greenwich Village, bought two of the pieces and took them "into town" (i.e., to the mainland, the city of Portland) to be framed. And those pictures are now the focus of inordinate admiration. What a difference that rather simple act of framing can make!

One of the most fundamental truisms of the art world is that a good frame calls no attention to itself, but only to the art that it surrounds. It does not change that piece of art in any way; it simply directs attention to it. And that is precisely what a good poet, or preacher, does. He or she puts a frame around a tiny piece of reality and cries, "Pay attention," cries "Look here!" cries, "This too is important, is significant, is crammed with meaning and with mystery, if you will just grant it a moment of your precious time." My poem "Fall Faith" describes a routine gardening chore in the fall of the year, and what this framing process might reveal.

Fall Faith

Today we combed the flower beds for Spring,
A father and two scavenging little girls,
Feeling among the fertile deaths of Fall
For next year's garden. Labeling our crop of gleanings
Into Fiona's extra Birth-Announcement envelopes.
P for Petunia, N for Nasturtium,
I—Impatiens, S—Snapdragon.

"See, this one has an ant in its mouth."
Small harvest heaps we built
Pods, motes, and corms, and curls,
Time capsules, May through August gaiety,
Granaried against another, unseen sun.

Thus faith, we pass it on from day to day.
Not listing, systematic presentation,
No catechismic, roting recitation of the "I believes."
A cellar work bench piled with
Fiona's extra Birth-Announcement envelopes,
P for Petunia, I—Impatiens,
S—Snapdragon . . .
Tokens, earnests, pledges sealed,
Outward and visible signs
of inward and spiritual hope,
Of warmth, of growth, of gaiety,
And of glory.[7]

Or again, a closer look at those exquisite creatures, hummingbirds, and the fascination that they exert on me every summer, disclosed at least a hint of the divine presence, as I describe it in my poem "Hummers."

Even in Maine's rain and fog I catch them,
often in pairs, or waiting, patient, perched on
a scarcely bending twig of our aged forsythia,
then working the window box petunias
till the coast seems clear, while I hover, motionless,
on the shadowed porch, hungry for still another glimpse
of ruby throat and emerald layered coat,
the delicate dip of beak in cup, the tilted head,
the blur of wings, that sudden flash of movement—
now-you-see-me-now-you-don't.

> Whatever it may be in me—
> some wandered/wondered child—
> that makes me watch and wait, this late,
> the daily hours to catch their, almost holy, visitations,
> I'm grateful for it, mindful too
> of one who every once in a long while, still hovers
> back there just beyond, behind the nearest edge
> of solitude, or prayer, or even glimpses
> of the tiniest of birds.[8]

This framing technique recalls the method Jesus used in his parables. He would take everyday phenomena—a lost sheep, a lost coin, a lost son—and by setting a frame around them, as it were, simply holding them up for focused and reflective attention, he revealed the dimension of the eternal there at the heart of the everyday. I have argued, in my devotional book *Seeing with the Soul— Daily Meditations on the Parables of Jesus in Luke*, that Jesus did not so much tell parables as he lived them, as he became himself a parable.[9] Parables were not mere illustrations for him, shedding indirect light on another, more important point. The parables themselves were the point. And the point they were making was that God, God's judgment and God's grace, God's beauty and God's power, God's kingdom or reign, all this is manifestly evident in everything that exists and in each event that happens around us. And all we need do is to stop, look, and listen, as he himself put it . . . to consider the lilies. It was Emily Dickinson, I believe, who once wrote in a letter to a friend that "consider the lilies of the field" was the one commandment she had never disobeyed. More than this,

Jesus' whole life was a parable, a frame around the thirty-some years of a humble country preacher who somehow got himself crucified. For this was a life that, when looked at, heeded and reflected upon, even prayed over, disclosed as never before the eternal love of God for God's human creation.

And this "parabling," as I have called it, is a process that must be continued and never stop. You and I as preachers have the responsibility of putting a frame around, calling attention to, not so much the spectacular things of this world (that was Jesus' temptation in the wilderness), not so much the dramatic and newsmaking stuff (it gets its own attention after all). Our job is to focus on the quotidian, the routine, the ordinary messy stuff that actually makes up most of what most of us call life, and to reveal the presence of eternity right there. It's our job to notice it, to find it and point it out. And if it's not there, if we can't find it, then we'd better find another job!

But the remarkable thing is that as, and whenever, we can find it—as and whenever we can disclose, reveal, God's grace within the everyday—we open up for our congregations the possibility that there may also be a parabolic dimension to their own lives; we invite and encourage them to join us in that poetic vision, that profound and imaginative reflection, that will reveal in due time what is really going on. Tom Troeger in his book *Imagining a Sermon* puts it this way:

> When we think about the parabolic nature of our lives in the light of God's word, we find patterns of meaning larger than ourselves. We locate the thread

of revelation that pulls us into the circle of the whole human family. And when we draw that thread of revelation into our sermons, then listeners begin to consider the parables of their own lives, and they become more attentive to where and how God is addressing them.[10]

Listen to Richard Wilbur parabling once again, as he sees laundry being hung out on a pulley early in the morning and moves on to reveal there the deepest meaning of incarnation and God's call to enfleshment. The poem is called, "Love Calls Us to the Things of This World."

> The eyes open to a cry of pulleys,
> And spirited from sleep, the astounded soul
> Hangs for a moment bodiless and simple
> As false dawn.
>   Outside the open window
> The morning air is all awash with angels.
>
>   Some are in bed-sheets, some are in blouses,
> Some are in smocks: but truly they are there.
> Now they are rising together in calm swells
> Of halcyon feeling, filling whatever they wear
> With the deep joy of their impersonal breathing;
>   Now they are flying in place, conveying
> The terrible speed of their omnipresence, moving
> And staying like white water; and now of a sudden
> They swoon down into so rapt a quiet
> That nobody seems to be there.
>   The soul shrinks
>
> From all that it is about to remember,
> From the punctual rape of every blessed day,
> And cries,
>   "Oh, let there be nothing on earth but laundry,
> Nothing but rosy hands in the rising steam

And clear dances done in the sight of heaven."
    Yet, as the sun acknowledges
With a warm look the world's hunks and colors,
The soul descends once more in bitter love
To accept the waking body, saying now
In a changed voice as the man yawns and rises,
    "Bring them down from their ruddy gallows;
Let there be clean linen for the backs of thieves;
Let lovers go fresh and sweet to be undone,
And the heaviest nuns walk in a pure floating
Of dark habits,
    Keeping their difficult balance."[11]

The Preacher's Task

Now faith is the assurance of things hoped for,
the conviction of things not seen.

Wallace Stevens in "The Necessary Angel" asks, "What is the poet's function?" And his reponse I would dare to apply also to the preacher:

What is his function? Certainly it is not to lead people out of the confusion in which they find themselves. Nor is it, I think, to comfort them while they follow their leaders to and fro. I think his function is to make his imagination theirs, and that he fulfils himself only as he sees his imagination become the light in the minds of others. . . . He has . . . immensely to do with giving life whatever savor it possesses.[12]

It has to do with what preachers and their kin might call "turning water into wine," or what Jesus himself decribed as being "the salt of the earth," a salt that must not "lose its savor." It has to do with a call to life that is more abundant, with that long-neglected experience we set out to look for as a treasure hunt, with the disclosure of sheer delight.

In the end, for me at least, it all goes back to that balcony in Bathgate High Church and that first answer in the Shorter Catechism:

Our chief end is to glorify God and enjoy God forever.

Loretta Ross-Gotta—a Presbyterian hermit, no less—writes:

The Church is long on edification but sometimes short on adoration. . . . We do not encourage or give opportunities to ourselves for much adoration. Adoration, the spontaneous, selfless expression of love for God, is our highest end and the task for which we have been created, according to the Westminster catechism.[13]

Praise and joy, adoration and delight. That, according to Julian Hartt, is finally what we are here for. He writes, "The Christian life is a resolute pursuit of ways in which to glorify God."[14] My poem "Clock Minder" links the chiming of an old clock in my study with the preacher's role in this glorification, this sounding forth of God's glory.

Clock Minder
I wind it every Sabbath before preaching,
retrieve the tarnished old brass key
from between its battered oaken feet,
flip open the glass face then turn

and turn the ratchet right,
recharging the tight coil to chart the falling springs
and springing falls that score the twining seasons—
two sockets for two windings, first the hands,
then the chimes—just as I climb the six steep steps
to launching off upon the most time-clad
yet time-defeating task ever was entrusted
to one formed of clay and spirit breath.

My calling too to tell—or toll—the hours,
remind how many and how few,
evoke a looking backward to review
before the leap ahead,
but also to resound, to echo forth a resonance
beneath and all around the measuring moments,
shape word and sound about a timelessness
that sings and soars the sonorous deeps
beyond the numbering of days.[15]

Praise as End and Goal

Now faith is the assurance of things hoped for,
the conviction of things not seen.

Walter Brueggemann in his Beecher Lectures stated that

praise is an act of poetry! It is only this poetry that will crack the muteness and let life begin again. . . . The preaching event is a modeling of praise, an act of lyrical articulation that breaks the muteness and shatters the deathly control in which our life is held. It is the task of the preacher to permit such praise, to summon to such praise, and to legitimate it. That task requires an enormous act of poetic imagination.[16]

Now I realize that praise, in the form of today's popular praise songs, may be a bit of a stretch for some of us. My homiletician friend Ernest Campbell calls them seven-eleven hymns, "seven words and eleven verses." The praise I have in mind is more akin to that of the Psalter, where time and again, amid the complaints, laments, recriminations, and cries for revenge, the note of praise breaks through until, in the last dozen psalms or so, all we get is pure praise. James Stewart, that prince of Scotland's preachers, put it this way:

> You have perhaps watched a great conductor bringing every member of his orchestra into action towards the close of some mighty music, have seen him, as the music climbed higher and higher, signalling to one player after another, and always at the signal another instrument responding to the summons and adding its voice to the music, until at the last crashing chords not one was left dumb, but all were uniting in a thrilling and triumphant climax. So these final psalms summon everything in creation to swell the glorious unison of God's praise. They signal to the sun riding in the heavens. "You come in now and praise Him!" Then to the myriad stars of night. "You now praise Him!"—then to the mountains, raking the clouds with their summits, "Praise Him!"—then to youth in all its strength and grace and beauty, "Praise Him!"—then to the kings and judges of the earth, "Praise Him!"—then to young manhood in its strength and maidenhood in its grace and beauty, "Praise Him!"—then to the multitude of saints in earth and heaven, "Praise Him!"—until the wide universe is shouting with every voice the praise of God alone. "While I live," cries the psalmist, "will

I praise the Lord: I will sing praises unto my God
while I have any being."[17]

One day a couple of Novembers ago I found myself,
just before midnight, in the deep silence of London's
Westminster Abbey, that shrine of England's history and
tradition. I was attending a dinner in the Jerusalem
Chamber adjoining the abbey, the room where Henry IV
was taken to die and where several centuries later the
Westminster Confession was hammered out. As the
evening wore on, I slipped from the table and, entering by
a narrow doorway, found myself alone in that soaring
nave, the tallest nave in Europe. Before me lay a bed of
scarlet poppies covering the tomb of Britain's unknown
soldier, for this was the eleventh day of the eleventh
month, the solemn anniversary of the armistice of the War
to End All Wars—World War I. All around me were the
emblems of mortality, the tombs of the great and the
good—poets and generals, statesmen, explorers, inven-
tors—with their fascinating inscriptions, their glowing
tributes.

I walked the length of that long aisle, along which
kings and queens had made their way to coronation, to
marriage, to interment. I stood a while before the great
high altar. And it seemed to me that all that I had seen
there—yes, the deaths and lives, the achievement and
insight, sheer courage, true faith—that all of this was
brought together here, embraced and lifted up to God,
lifted up in one great hymn of thanks and praise and
glory. And I saw that that's what we are called to do, that
this is where the treasure hunt is leading in the end. To

perceive and then reach out toward the best that is in all of us, to welcome it, rejoice in it, and claim it, own it—yes, in Christ's name—recognize it for what it truly is, the love and grace of God at work. And then lift it up, yes, raise it high in praise and thanks to God, God the source and God the goal.

What a calling! What a splendid and fully delightful vocation! To perceive and then show forth God's grace in action and God's glory. To call forth and rejoice in, delight in, the gifts, the manifold graces our Creator and Redeemer has hidden here and there; that God with the divine image (the *imago Dei*) has concealed within us and around us, all there to be discovered.

Of course, it's not always easy or necessarily delightful; that goes without saying. It may often be joyful, but that's a biblical joy we're talking about, and therefore often, in hymn writer George Matheson's words, a "joy that seekest (us) through pain." Auden, in his Christmas Oratorio *For the Time Being,* calls us in those long post-Christmas weeks and months to the daily chore of practicing "our scales of rejoicing." That certainly adds a new dimension to the phrase, "a practicing Christian."

It may not always be easy, but it is what we are called to, what we have been given to work with, for the time being. Leonard Cohen—not exactly my favorite poet, but then the muse is much more egalitarian than we tend to be—has words in his song "Anthem" that have haunted me of late, words that, in their modestly realistic aspiration toward glory, point us once again, in closing, in the direction of delight:

Ring the bells that still can ring.
Forget your perfect offering.
There is a crack, a crack in everything.
That's how the light gets in.
That's where the light gets in.

Chapter 5

DELIGHT IN ACTION

❧❧❦❦

In this final chapter, as mentioned in the introduction, I am offering three sermons, preached on various occasions, selected here as somewhat typical examples of my own attempts at living out some of the advice and counsel offered in the preceding pages.

Nothing Matters![1]

This first sermon employs an element of play and surprise as it seeks profound meaning in the somewhat alien concept of nothingness. I also draw on the arts and science for illustrative material and use a pair of French quotations (with translation) and even a quote from Heidegger, which would not be appropriate, of course, in every setting, but fit well within a sermon preached at Yale University's Battell Chapel. There are also personal narratives here: walking in the New Hampshire woods, listening to a concert, visiting Walden Pond. There are those who counsel the avoidance of all such personal material in the pulpit. For my part, such incidents provide living testimony to one of my own most primary convictions, the presence of the divine at the heart of everyday, ordinary, even personal reality.

❧❧❦❦

Let these words that I speak,
and the thoughts we all think,
bring us closer to you, O God,
nearer to one another. Amen.

In Isaiah, chapter 40, verse 17:

All the nations are as nothing before God, they are accounted as less than nothing and emptiness.

And in 1 Corinthians, chapter 1, verse 28 (RSV):

God chose what is low and despised in the world, even things that are not, to bring to nothing things that are.

"My paintings are about nothing," a rather successful artist in my former congregation in Greenwich Village wrote to me. "My paintings are about nothing"—thus triggering a train of thought that led toward the realization that, in an odd and rather intriguing way, my own poetry, my preaching too, is really about nothing. Hence my title for this morning: "Nothing Matters."

That artist went on to say that the empty spaces between the images in his paintings—"the intellectual distances" he called them—were at least as important as the images themselves. Just four weeks ago I heard the Philadelphia Orchestra play the young Scottish composer James Macmillan's *Third Symphony*, subtitled "Silence." And those silences—don't you see?—those at times crashing silences that punctuated his music, were every bit as eloquent, as haunting, as the melodies, harmonies, chords, even discords that emerged out of those silences. Henri Nouwen has written:

> Silence is the home of the word. Silence gives strength and fruitfulness to the word. We can even say that words are meant to disclose the mystery of the silence from which they come.[2]

Or, as I read on a little three-by-five card pinned to the wall of a medieval abbey at Conques in southern France:

> *Le bruit ne fait pas de bien.*
> *Le bien ne fait pas de bruit.*

> Noise doesn't do any good.
> Good doesn't make any noise.

Ask any dramatist, any actor, about the pauses, the caesuras— any poet, for that matter. Ask about those moments in their work when nothing happens, nothing is heard, and you may begin to understand why nothing matters. Empty spaces, vacant lots, black holes, broad margins around, within our art, our thought, our very existence. Nothing matters.

Nothing matters in the first place, let me propose, because there just might be something there. In the sciences of late, have you noticed, a growing number of researchers are focusing upon nothing. Or put it this way: rather than seeking to expand what we already know, concentrating on the body of knowledge already gathered and trying to increase it, to expand the frontiers; some scientists have begun focusing way out there, on the unknown, upon what we cannot yet, and may, indeed, never be able to explain.

Beware of making things too comprehensible—one of the as yet largely unrealized perils of our age. Beware of making things too comprehensible. For the easier we make things to understand, the greater the risk of not understanding at all. A recent newspaper article under the heading "Dumbed Down Shakespeare" reported on the latest methods for teaching literature in some of our schools. Here's a verse or two in case you missed it:

But soft! What light through yonder window breaks?

is translated for benighted readers of today into

But wait! What light is coming from that window?

While

To be, or not to be: that is the question:
Whether 'tis nobler in the mind to suffer
The slings and arrows of outrageous fortune,
Or to take arms against a sea of troubles,
And by opposing end them.

now reads:

To be, or not to be; that is what really matters.
Is it nobler to accept passively
the trials and tribulations that unjust fate sends,
or to resist an ocean of troubles,
and, by our own effort, defeat them?

And they've done this—they're still doing it—to the Bible!
Now I realize much of what is done to the Scriptures today is the result of new and improved scholarship. But more than a few of the most recent versions come perilously close to easy

114

readin'. And if you're not sure what I mean by that, try tuning your car radio to one of those "easy listenin' stations," and I think you'll get it. Do people not see that they are taking the discomfort, the unknown, the mystery—yes, the nothing—out of the Scriptures, and leaving them so facile, so smooth, so easy to comprehend that they are hardly worth reading any more, because they hold no heights and depths, no subtlety, no paradox; in short, because they tell us nothing we do not already know?

Yes, nothing matters in the first place, because as we look at nothing, as we contemplate that which appears to be empty, meaningless, null and void, there is no telling what truths may emerge. Nothing matters because there just may be something there.

In the second place, let me suggest that nothing matters because there may even be everything there. The routine and the predictable dominate so much of what we do today, who we are, how we pass our time. We spend our days, our work, our leisure too, with what is immediate and to hand, what is familiar, old hat, and therefore safe. It's how we survive, how we maintain our sanity. But might there be more at stake than sanity? "Our mind has lost itself in the world" cries Rabbi Abraham Heschel. We become so taken up with the here and the now, Heschel observes, so preoccupied with all that is given and assumed, the accumulated preconceptions of our daily routines and of our society, that anything beyond is considered to be what the rabbi calls "an illegitimate fancy." We become, in other words, bogged down in our own footprints.

Walking in the deep snow of the New Hampshire woods a couple of winters ago, with Dugal, our tiny, four-pound Yorkshire terrier, at my heels. Suddenly the little dog was missing, nowhere to be seen, until, retracing my steps, I found him huddled at the bottom of one of my own bootprints, trapped in a sheer hole of ice with no way to clamber out. So too we become caught in our own footsteps, trapped within the chill and empty dailyness of one-damn-thing-after-another.

There still are those gaps, of course, those glimpses of nothingness; we are all of us granted such moments, snatches, visions—I am persuaded of that. But we fear them most of the time, we flee them, because they tell us far more than we want to know, they tell us everything—who we are, where we are going—they remind us of our limits, our finitude, yes, our death. *Et loin de nous, peut être,* writes Sully Prudhomme:

> *Et loin de nous, peut être, . . . l'ombre de l'ombre humaine existe, et fait de l'ombre.*[3]

> And far distant from us, perhaps, the shadow of the human shadow exists, and casts a shadow.

And yet . . . and yet, that is also the way to life. Heidegger it was who argued that "it is only through confrontation with the nothing that for the first time we become seized of the wonder of Being." Thomas Merton writes of the contemplative life as "an advance into solitude and the desert, a confrontation with poverty and the void, a renunciation of the empirical self, in the presence of death, and nothingness, in order to overcome the ignorance and error that spring from the fear of 'being nothing.' "[4] While our Lord himself, Jesus, spoke repeatedly, more often than any other saying in the Gospels, of finding life in the very act of giving it away.

> The one who would save his life will lose it. But whoever will lose his life, for my sake and the gospels, that one will find it forever. (Mark 8:35, au. trans.)

Nothing matters. No thing—don't you see?—no actual, physical thing ultimately matters. There are no pockets in a shroud. And in this possessive, consumptive, object-ownership-obsessed world, there is a desperate need for time and space, opportunity to contemplate nothing, to contemplate no thing; for nothing matters.

During a preaching visit to Harvard some years ago, we took a drive out to Walden Pond in order to contemplate nothing. But between the ticket seller at the entrance to the parking lot, the ice cream and hot dog wagon, the "Shop at Walden Pond" run by the Thoreau Society where one can purchase colorful Walden T-shirts—one of them actually read, "Beware of all occasions for which you have to buy new clothes"—and then the Walden Society newsletter, rather cutely called *The Ponder;* surrounded by all these *things,* we didn't have much time. It was that other Massachusetts mystic, Emily Dickinson, who wrote,

> To make a prairie it takes a clover and one bee,
> One clover, and a bee,
> And revery.
> The revery alone will do,
> If bees are few.[5]

Nothing matters!

One final thing: if we look at nothing, if we have the courage and the faith to look away once in a while from everything, all those things that dominate our consciousness, our motivation and ambition, even our dreams; if we will look deep into the nothing that informs us of our finitude and death, we will find God there. That is the testimony of the ages. That is the message of the monks and mystics, those whose lives have claimed, staked out the time to venture into timelessness. What was it that Paul wrote to those Corinthians?

> God chose what is low and despised in the world, even things that are not, to bring to nothing things that are.
> (1 Cor. 1:28 RSV)

And Job, Elijah, Isaiah too, faced with the destruction of everything they cherished, found at the heart of that nothingness no bleak emptiness but a God—a God so vast as to shape the universe, so intimate as to reason with and wrestle with, to live for and ultimately die for the life of God's human creation.

Those gaps, yes, in art, music, poetry; those moments in daily life, both tragedy and joy, when the world seems to drop away, and nothing, no thing is left before you: can you learn, can we begin to see them not as gaping holes but as gateways, not as abysses but as avenues toward new insight, new wisdom, new glimpses into the height and depth of grace? Whether it be "like an open door, or like an open wound," writes Brother David,

> Be it like an open door, or an open wound, the heart of man
> is that point of the world which is open toward Mystery.[6]

Nothing matters.

The tale is told of a tired, city-weary man who rented a riverfront cabin in the country. Meeting him on the porch, the owner looked him over thoughtfully. Then he said:

> Now be careful, and if you want a good stay here, remember what I'm going to tell you. Sit on this deck facing downstream for as long as you need. Don't look upstream, keep your face downstream. Let the river carry everything away. Let it empty you. It may take days. Only when it has emptied you, will you be ready to turn your chair and face upstream. And when you do, let the river flow into you and fill you.

Then, as he turned to leave, he added:

> And don't you be too quick to turn your chair around. When you first think you're ready, most likely you're not!

Nothing matters. No thing matters. Nothing . . . *matters!* A call to contemplation, a call to meditation, a call to reevaluation. A call to life.

Let us pray.

Lord God, let no thing,
no physical object or concern,
come between us and the life you offer in Jesus Christ.
Teach us to confront the nothing of our life and death,
and then to find the grace, sheer grace, of everything,
even eternal life in Christ our Lord.
Amen.

My Way or the Highway![7]

This sermon, preached in a suburban parish church in the Washington, D.C., area, reaches toward the realms of politics, as well as theology. It tackles a topic that I am convinced troubles the faith of many believers, but is all too often ignored by preachers: the fierce note of condemnation that runs through much of our Holy Scriptures. In doing so, it also questions the readiness of our political leaders to divide the world into those who are with us, or against us. I suspect that the illustration of the lynching of Mussolini may be pushing things a bit for some, but I did encourage us to be daring and to give people something to argue about afterwards. Again, at the climax of the sermon, I turn to a personal vein, both with the incident driving in Virginia and with the birthday reflections at the close. I make no apologies for this. My preaching grows out of my life in the faith, and my own wrestling with that faith. If that lifelong struggle had to be excluded, then my sermons would be lifeless.

❧❧❧❧

> In this time set apart from time,
> this holy moment halfway to eternity,
> give us the faith to truly listen for your voice,
> give us the wisdom to discern
> what you would have us do and be,
> and grant us the inner peace
> of knowing we are ever in your hands. Amen.

My text is from the first psalm, the fourth verse:

> The wicked are not so,
> but are like chaff which the wind drives away. (RSV)

I met a movie star in New York a couple of years ago. We were at a party and, not being much of a moviegoer, I had little idea of what he actually did. "I tend to play the villains," he told me, "the bad guys, those characters the audiences love to hate." And then he gave a grin, a sort of sideways, sort of teeth-baring grin, and his friendly, handsome, rather striking face was transformed for an instant, and I glimpsed what all those audiences must have seen there. He was a charming person actually, an active layman, much involved in the life of a struggling inner-city parish, and we had a good discussion about the dimensions and demands of urban ministry. But I left there intrigued; I had finally met an honest-to-God villain, a professional villain at that!

Who are these wicked ones the Psalms go on so much about? Where can we find the reprobates, degenerates, those so regularly and enthusiastically condemned in these Scriptures? Because, make no mistake about it, for all our talk of forgiveness nowadays, this Bible spells out, often in lurid detail, the fate of those who reject the ways and will of God. As we read in the First Psalm:

> Therefore the wicked will not stand in the judgment,
>   nor sinners in the congregation of the righteous;
> for the LORD knows the way of the righteous,
>   but the way of the wicked will perish. (RSV)

Yes, it's *My Way, or the Highway,* says the Lord.

And it's not just in the Psalms. Throughout this Bible—the New Testament every bit as much as the Old—we find the same thing: judgment, condemnation, eternal punishment decreed for all who reject God's grace, even for those, according to some passages, who do so unwittingly, who have never even heard of Christ, let alone rejected him.

Even Jesus, our compassionate Savior, who gave his life that none should be condemned, according to the Gospel writers seems to have balanced his words of compassion and forgiveness with words about weeping, wailing, and the gnashing of teeth.

> Then [God] will say to those at his left hand, "Depart from me, you cursed, into the eternal fire prepared for the devil and his angels; for I was hungry and you gave me no food, I was thirsty and you gave me no drink, I was a stranger and you did not welcome me, naked and you did not clothe me, sick and in prison and you did not visit me. (Matt. 25:41–43 RSV)

Those majestic scenes—you may have seen some of them—carved in elaborate detail above the doors of the great cathedrals across Europe as a warning to all who enter, scenes of the Last Judgment, in which the elect on the one side are ushered into eternal bliss, and the damned on the other side (and there are usually far more of them, and they are depicted with much more gusto) are seized by gleeful devils and pitchforked into the furnaces of hell. What do we do with all those biblical passages that separate the sheep from the goats, the good guys from the bad, those stories—yes, doctrines too— that inculcate the belief that while we are all God's children, some of us nevertheless, a good many of us indeed, are going to suffer forever in Hades?

Of course, it's not just Christianity and the Bible that teach this. I suspect we would be hard pressed to find any religion, any culture or civilization, that has not, in some way or another, separated humanity into us and them, the chosen and the rejected, the saved and the damned. That's how our thinking—our basic understanding of who we are—goes, has gone from the beginning. The goodies and the baddies, cops and robbers, cowboys and outlaws, Allies and Nazis, the free world and Marxists, the coalition of the willing and the axis of evil . . . so it goes.

Maybe that's all right with you, just so long as we assign the categories correctly. Maybe there really are just two kinds of people: us and that other kind who deserve everything they get. But I have learned over the years to be suspicious when people start talking in such terms. One thing I look out for is just where such speakers place themselves. And I've yet to hear one who believed that he or she belonged among the damned. As that great Scot John Baillie once put it:

> Had the doctrine (of Hell) been worked out, from the beginning and steadily, in terms of what its proponents felt *themselves* to deserve, it would have to be taken very seri-

ously; but in fact it bears the taint of having been worked out in terms of what its proponents felt to be the deserts of their neighbors, or rather, of their enemies. And except when we begin to reflect on our own merits, our human thinking is never so prone to err as when we begin to reflect on our neighbour's defects.[8]

"Evil is never more quietly powerful than in the assumption that it resides elsewhere," wrote Chicago theologian Joseph Sittler. And surely the cause of, or at least the justification for, the vast majority of those crimes against humanity we have defiled ourselves with throughout our history—from concentration camps to carpet bombing to ethnic cleansing—has been rooted in this claim to be fighting on the side of God against the forces of evil incarnate.

Now perhaps I'm just a *bleeding-heart liberal,* one of those softhearted, not to say softheaded types, so protected from the real world of violence and crime that I cannot bear the thought of anyone being punished. But as I read these Scriptures, the *whole* of them, not just isolated and at times ambiguous fragments; as I study the *overall* message of this Bible; as I grapple to work out the fullest implications of our incarnation-based faith—that alarmingly humble manger birth, that grace lived out in healing, teaching, and forgiving, that horrendous death, that implausible and yet insistent resurrection—as I struggle with all this, I find it more and more impossible to divide our human race, to separate the good from the bad in this drastic, yes, ultimate, way.

Maybe part of the problem is that I don't know anybody, never have encountered anyone, who is all that good—I mean so much better than the next person that they deserve eternal bliss, while the other burns in hell. One of the promises held out to the blessed, one of the rewards actually promised in sermons of not too long ago to those who followed Christ's way, was the prospect of ringside seats at the inferno, the delight of watching as spectators from the ramparts of heaven while those who didn't make the cut suffered eternal torment below. Indeed, we find this very prospect in the Psalms. "Only with thine eyes shalt thou behold and see the reward of the wicked," promises the writer of that otherwise sublime Psalm 91 (v. 8 KJV). We have a name for folk like that nowadays; we call them sadists. And I can think of nothing further removed from what I believe to be the fullness and the grace of Christ's gospel.

Not only have I never met anyone who was all that good, I've never yet met anyone wicked enough to deserve eternal torment either. How does that little rhyme go again?

> There is so much *good* in the *worst* of us,
> And so much bad in the best of us,
> That it hardly becomes any of us
> To talk about the rest of us.

Oh, yes, we have our fiends—our Hitlers, Stalins and the rest, and nowadays we'd better add Osama and Saddam to the list—and perhaps if I had been the victim of one of these, held captive in a gulag or shot and then shoveled into a mass grave, I could summon up sufficient hatred to wish eternal torment upon them. But I would not be proud of such emotion. That would not be the best of me speaking. Indeed that would involve lowering myself to their level. And I could not believe in or love a God who spoke for the worst in me, who gave voice and promised fulfillment to the most vengeful and base of my emotions.

When that mob seized Mussolini in the waning days of World War II, tore him from his cell, battered him, slashed at his body, and then hanged him—upside down, wasn't it?—in the public square, the Piazzale Lareto in Milan, you might argue they were only administering long-delayed justice to a grotesque tyrant. But that's not the justice I expect from the God and Father of our Lord Jesus Christ. And that brutalized, degraded, humiliated figure on those Italian gallows—fifty-nine, was it? years ago now—whatever his crimes, looks uncomfortably like another child of God who was stripped, flogged, and nailed on a tree to die.

Surely if that cross tells us one thing, it says we were all involved: the powers of state and church, the compliance of the mob, the apathy of the respectable, the betrayal and flight of supporters and friends. Where were the goodies and the baddies at that moment? Who was on the Lord's side, when our Lord gave up his life for you and me? You tell me, you show me where they are, because I haven't been able to find them.

So we are all sinners, all failures; we all deny, betray, sell out, choose fear over love, keep silent or get lost in the crowd rather than risk body, status, life itself for what is true, good, and beautiful. We're all going to hell—let's face it—we're every one of us doomed if it takes an act of genuine, uncomplicated, un-mixed-motivated love to get us out of there. And wouldn't you know it, that is precisely what it did take—precisely what it did take. And since none of us could do it, since not one human being was capable of such an act, he showed us how. He lived it out and died it out for us. He took that age-old, unending cycle of violence and revenge, of crime and retribution, of grudge, resentment, and vendetta, and he broke it, sliced clean through the chain that has bound us since the days of Cain and Abel, and simply said, "The buck stops here; yes, the hate, the bloodshed, and the hurt, all the condemnation that has been passed down and down forever, stops right here at this cross. I take it all upon myself. I'll pay the price. I'll be the one condemned. And after that, no one else need be. You will have a fresh start, a new creation."

"There is therefore now no condemnation," writes Paul in Romans (Rom. 8:1 RSV), and again in 2 Corinthians:

> For the Son of God, Jesus Christ, whom we preached among
> you . . .
> was not Yes and No; but in him it is always Yes.
> For all the promises of God find their Yes in him.
>   2 Cor. 1:19–20 RSV

In some thirty-eight years of preaching and studying the Word of God, I am more and more convinced that Jesus came, not to tell us who is going to heaven and who is going to hell, but to offer, and offer, and offer again, to each and every one of us, life, abundant life, life that is truly eternal and that begins right here, right now.

Driving home through rural Virginia a couple of years ago now, returning along the Eastern Shore from welcoming a new grandchild born on Easter Day, I caught, out of the corner of one eye, one of those religious billboards that are so plentiful in that area. I groaned inwardly, expecting the kind of self-righteous, judgmental message I have learned to expect from such sources, but slowed down to read it just the same. Here is what I read: "The heart, generous and kind, most resembles God." And I said a little prayer of thanksgiving for a God who still manages to surprise us, to shock us, to blindside us, with an eternally compassionate grace.

This is the grace, the undying love, the divine compassion we meet at the cross—a compassion that will not, cannot condemn any one of God's own children, but gives itself, and gives itself forever, in sacrificial and in the end triumphantly redeeming love.

The wicked are not so,
but are like chaff which the wind drives away.

Can we do away with the wicked once for all—at least the wicked as those people out there, over there, locked up in there, wherever? "Evil," as Lance Morrow puts it in his just-published book *Evil—An Investigation,* in words that desperately need to be taken to heart by our current political leadership, "Evil is a . . . versatile and dangerous word that can be used to describe a genocide or to incite one."

What was it Paul said in our reading? "Let us not therefore judge one another any more" (Rom. 14:13 KJV). Next Wednesday, Ash Wednesday, I will enter my seventieth year as I observe my sixty-ninth birthday. There are, it is said, two ways of looking at birthdays: as a deadline, or as a lifeline; as a grim reminder of how much time has gone by and how little has been achieved, or as a thankful celebration of God's continuing gift of life. For the Christian church, of course, every Sunday is a birthday, a rebirth day, the Day of Resurrection. On this birthday, then, this day of celebration of new life in Jesus Christ, can we begin at last to acknowledge what we have always known in our most honest heart of hearts, that the dividing line between good and evil does not run down the middle of society, separating good person from bad, good neighbor from bad, good nation, good race, good politics, good religion, good sexual orientation from bad? Let's stop tearing ourselves, and each other, apart and leave that kind of judgment in God's hands where it belongs; "Judgment is mine, I will repay," says the Lord. No, that line, that dividing line between good and evil, runs down the center of your being and my being, of your immortal soul and mine. And then let us give thanks for the grace of Christ we still find revealed in one another—yes, for all our various faults and foibles—that surprising, undefeated grace that still works and struggles and every so often even triumphs within each and every one of us, and go forth as fellow saints and fellow sinners, to seek out the steps of Christ, the royal paths of love, the sovereign ways of mercy and forgiveness, so that *My Way* becomes at last *The Highway,* and we can walk that way together as children of one Father, the people of one God.

Let us pray:

Teach us, Lord Christ, about right and wrong,
about good and bad, about friend and foe;
then lead us by your grace into the family of faith,
that family that embraces one and all within the mystery of
hope,
within the economy of love. Amen.

Seeing Is Believing[9]

In this sermon, preached at morning worship during the 2004 General Assembly of the Presbyterian Church (U.S.A.), my goal was to break away from the guilt/sin/redemption complex that dominates so much of Western Christianity and reach toward a more sacramental theology, in which Christ is the one who reveals the presence and the grace of God in every aspect of God's creation—the parabolic understanding that I outlined in chapter 4. Once again the sermon is built around, not only the biblical witness, but also the experience of my own life—memories of child-hood, a stay in the hospital, a trip to my native Scotland. In this way I am again seeking to demonstrate the "parabolic" nature of our days, God's presence "in, with, and under" the routine of the everyday.

❊❊❊❊

Stretch us, O God, in this hour.
Draw out all of the kinks, the knots, the cramps and creases,
all the weary, fearful, timid places of our souls,
and shape us into something new, something beyond,
something brimming, spilling, running over with abundant
    life.
Let us be born, be born anew, in Christ. Amen.

John, the ninth chapter and the second verse (NRSV):

> Rabbi, who sinned, this man or his parents,
> that he was born blind?

"Father! Mother! I can see!" Words once memorized, never forgotten. The very first words, in fact, that I ever spoke in church, at age ten or eleven (was it?), playing the part, in a Sunday school drama, of that same blind man in John's Gospel.
    Father! Mother! I can see!
Maybe it's all about seeing.
    So they meet a man blind from birth, and the disciples ask Jesus whose fault it is. They don't ask him to heal the man. They're just curious. They want to know who is responsible for this unfortunate condition. And, as he heals him anyway, Jesus tells them they are asking entirely the wrong question; he was not born blind because of his own sin or that of his parents, but to provide an opportunity to show the power of God.
    Those disciples—don't you see?—were playing the old blame game. They wanted to know whose fault it was. They needed some kind of reasonable allocation of guilt, so they could say he's blind because of this or that, this harmful action, that sinful person. But Jesus said it was all about manifesting God's glory, and just went ahead and healed the man.

We too persist in looking for someone to blame. We too would rather call a thing a curse of God—a fitting punishment for some previous fault or crime—than ever admit that such things just happen, might even happen to us. We too insist on seeking out the guilty party, the one in the wrong, that individual, community, or nation that is different from us, that sees things from an opposite perspective, and thus can be blamed for whatever currently troubles us.

But what Jesus seems to suggest is that instead of asking whom to blame, those disciples should have been asking whom to praise, whom to glorify: "Just whose is the glory involved?" Perhaps, in other words, the appropriate approach to this world—its mysteries, quandaries, tragedies, and comedies too—the correct, even the Christian approach, is not so much that of guilt, as that of glory. Let me try to explain.

Two weeks ago I was discharged after eight long days in Portland's Maine Medical Center fighting a tenacious infection. While confined I escaped the weariest moments via a series of paperback mysteries—those British "police procedurals"—in which Inspector Morse, or Rebus or whoever, engages in the relentless investigation of a crime, invariably murder, so that every moment, event, conversation, even every piece of local landscape, becomes a potential clue, and the whole world becomes a crime scene.

At the very same time, beyond my hospital window, there spread the lakes and woods of Maine stretching as far as the White Mountains, with Mount Washington outlined against the sunset. And there I lay: my head, when it was clear enough, caught up in a fascinating fantasy world of pursuit, prosecution, and punishment; my eyes, when they were clear enough, delighting in the God-given splendor of creation. But, you know, when it came right down to healing . . . the eyes had it!

That radiant vista fed my soul, lifted me beyond all the IV tubes, pills, probes, and catheters, into the reality of a God of majesty, mystery, and grace.

. What if seeing really was believing? What if we could learn to look at life, and even faith, that way? Not as a crime scene, where we are forever asking what is wrong, what's missing, what doesn't add up, and who is to blame, but as a scene of wonder, a transformation scene, in which, by careful, prayerful looking, we discern signs of God's presence, God's healing power, God's astonishing, even terrifying beauty.

In other words, suppose that Jesus came to teach us how to see? So often in the Gospels, especially in John, from his earliest invitation, "Come and see," to his opening the eyes of the blind, his naming himself as "the light of the world," all those parables, so many of which were simple exercises in seeing, in perceiving the reality of God concealed in everyday events and objects—something lost, a coin, a sheep, a son, a farmer sowing seed, a traveler needing help—in all this, Jesus seems to be inviting people to a new way of seeing, a new way of discerning, of recognizing God and God's realm at the core of everything that is.

To approach this world, this life, then, no longer as a problem to be solved, but as a possibility to be explored. To approach and appreciate our own selves, no longer as defined exclusively between those two opposing poles of sin and salvation, but as those who, being redeemed in Christ, can now seek out, recognize, and reveal to others the living splendor of that redemption, its passion, its surpassing glory, reflected in the world about us, at work in the events that shape our time.

In my retirement—and it's a splendidly liberating thing this retirement, particularly if your pension is fully vested—in reflecting upon thirty-eight-plus years of ordained ministry, I am becoming more and more convinced that Western Christianity, at least, has become obsessed with sin and guilt, an obsession that has led to the neglect, at times the denial, of other equally biblical areas of theology: creation, the Spirit, the church, history, justice, community, to name a few. And this obsession, it seems to me, is rooted in a deeply ambivalent attitude toward sexuality. So many of us, after all, came to the faith as teenagers, while wrestling with the explosive emergence of our own selves as sexual beings.

Something's wrong somewhere; something . . . someone is shameful. And since that shameful person cannot finally be me, it must be someone else: the alien, the minority person, the woman, the Muslim or Jew, the gay person; the fault has to lie somewhere. So, as with Inspector Morse, the world becomes one vast crime scene, and our task is to locate the guilty party. And as long as folk see the world that way, then someone, somewhere, has to take the blame.

> Rabbi, who sinned, this man or his parents,
> that he was born blind?

Theologian H. Richard Niebuhr in his later works expressed a growing concern over what he called the "Christomonism" of the West. By this he meant our tendency to narrow the faith down to a single, simplistic, and quite unbiblical focus on the second person of the Trinity alone, to the exclusion of the richness, depth, and comprehensive breadth of Christian thought across the ages.

Today we face an even further narrowing, a narrowing down to something we might call "sin-omonism," "guilt-omonism," maybe even "forgiveness-omonism," a narrowing in which the focus is so exclusively upon the cross—just look at Mel Gibson's *Passion*—and the most rigid transactional interpretation of what happened on that cross, that the full spectrum, that radiant, rainbow range by which our faith has been able to encompass and embrace the entirety of creation and the cosmos, has been almost completely forfeited.

I said "unbiblical" just now fully realizing that there is much in Scripture to support this view of God as the fearsome judge in whose presence our only possible act must be to grovel in confession. Yet a fully biblical view, a view that encompasses Abraham, for one, the exemplar of our faith, who argues with God over the fate of Sodom; Jacob, who wrestles with the mystery that is and is not God, and then limps into the sunrise; Koheleth, the preacher; David, the psalmist too; and then Job—surely the whole point of Job is his sinlessness, and when he finally does submit, it is not the result of guilt, but of God's sheer mystery and splendor—yes, a *fully* biblical view would lend support to a far richer and fuller range of relationship with the divine than can ever be defined solely by that first verse of John Newton's "Amazing Grace."

Those crowds who flocked to Jesus, and the winsome, winning message Jesus fed to them: oh yes, there was repentance there, but repentance in the fullest sense of the Hebrew Scriptures, a transformation of one's entire being, a turning full around (*shub* is the Hebrew word), a realization and recognition that this truly is "our Father's world" and that everything in it, from bushel baskets to pearls of great price, speaks and even sings to us of glory, if we would only stop and look and listen.

Do you remember how they asked Jesus why his followers behaved so differently from those of the Baptist with his austere warnings to "flee from the wrath to come." What happened to us, that so much of his church, even today, is still hanging with John the Baptist, rather than rejoicing with the risen Lord of the Dance?

You Christians should look more redeemed.

So said Nietzsche—a pastor's son, by the way—in one of his most telling criticisms of our church.

Now don't let anyone claim that I am denying the reality of sin or questioning the necessity of the cross. What I am saying is that there is even more to our faith than this, that we have other, *further* songs to sing, that we are heirs of a glorious heritage—of sin and grace, yes, but also of gratitude and glory, of mystery and wonder, of a God whose majesty transcends even that revealed by the Hubbell telescope, yet who is also, in the poet's words,

Closer . . . than breathing, and nearer than hands and feet.[10]

Last May Mhairi and I visited Roslin Chapel. For a tiny village just south of Scotland's capital city, Roslin has recently come upon at least two claims to fame. First, it is the birthplace, or rather the cloning place, of Dolly the infamous sheep. Second, we find here the chapel whose stunning architecture, I am told, plays a major role in that blockbuster bestseller *The Da Vinci Code*. I had actually set out to visit the chapel years before—it dates from the fifteenth century—but had never been able to find it. Anyway, last May we stood there in wonder. It is a tiny place, really, for a church, and yet every available square centimeter of stone is decorated, encrusted with the most splendid and elaborate carving—not only biblical scenes, but the heroes and legends of classical mythology. One glimpses all kinds of animals, fruit, and flowers, including, quite amazingly, an archway of maize carved well before Columbus reached the New World. Peeking out here and there, almost concealed among the vines, one finds the grinning, pagan face of the green man, one of northern Europe's most ancient fertility figures. Even death, in all its medieval starkness, dances its bony way along the pillars and window frames.

Visitors were invited to enter prayer requests in a book on a stand, and I wrote in the name of a close and dear relative recently diagnosed with a brain tumor. Then, promptly at noon, we were gently invited to worship God. And all that vast cornucopia of life—nature and history, legend and imagination, the seven deadly sins, even old death itself—yes, all we know and wonder at was lifted up, along with those names, in praise and prayer and honest gratitude to God.

And I saw that that's what we are called to do . . . "Father, Mother, I can see!" To perceive, recognize, and then reach out toward the very best that is in all of us, and all creation too; to welcome it, rejoice in it, and claim it, own it—yes, in Christ's name—recognize it for what it truly is, the love and grace of our God at work. And then lift it up, yes, raise it high, in praise to God the source and God the goal.

Guilt, then, or glory? A church of separation: sorting out the guilty from the good, the chosen from the frozen, poring over these Scriptures to discern who's in and who's out? Or a church of celebration: seeking out God's realm in every moment of our living, yes, the sad every bit as much as the glad; looking for, believing in, seeking ever to bring to light and nurture, that image of God that still lies deep in the human heart, that makes every single one of us worth Christ's dying for. Oh, we are flawed and fragile creatures, to be sure, and yet by means of these very flaws we can be shaped, shaped to the life of Christ. In his song "Anthem," the poet Leonard Cohen puts it this way:

Ring the bells that still can ring.
forget your perfect offering.
There is a crack, a crack in everything.
That's how the light gets in.
That's where the light gets in . . . . Amen.

Notes

Front Matter

1. This invocation was written for the annual meeting of the Presbyterian Writers' Guild, held during the 212th General Assembly of the Presbyterian Church (U.S.A.) in Fort Worth, TX, in June of 1999.

Chapter 1: A Death of Delight

1. Rubem A. Alves, *The Poet, the Warrior, the Prophet,* Edward Cadbury Lectures 1990 (London: SCM Press, and Philadelphia: Trinity Press International, 1990), 130.
2. H. A. Williams, *True Resurrection* (London and New York: Continuum, 2000), 97.
3. Kathleen Norris, "Amazing Grace," *Riverhead Trade* (April 1, 1999): 71.
4. Samuel H. Miller, *The Life of the Soul* (New York: Phoenix Press, Walker & Co., 1986), 98.
5. Barbara Brown Taylor, *When God Is Silent* (Boston: Cowley Publications, 1998), 39.
6. Walter Brueggemann, *Finally Comes the Poet—Daring Speech for Proclamation* (Minneapolis: Fortress Press, 1989).
7. Ibid., 3.
8. Ibid., 88.
9. Ibid.,109.
10. Alves, *The Poet, the Warrior, the Prophet,* 7.
11. Cited by Paul Brooks in "Out of Mind," a column in *Prospect* magazine. May 2002.
12. T. S. Eliot, *On Poetry and Poets* (New York: Noonday Press of Farrar, Straus & Giroux, 1961), 14.
13. Alves, *The Poet, the Warrior, the Prophet,* 101. Henri Nouwen narrates a similar incident from the life of

Beethoven, who, when asked of a new sonata, "What does it mean?" simply returned to the piano and played it again (*The Genesee Diary* [New York: Doubleday, Image, 1981], 37f.)

14. From an address to the Covenant Network of the Presbyterian Church (U.S.A.), November 3, 2001, Pasadena Presbyterian Church, Pasadena, CA.
15. *Christian Century*, April 14, 1993.
16. Gerald Stern, "American Sonnets" (New York, London: W. W. Norton & Co., 2002), 27.
17. Matthew Fox, "Meditations with Meister Eckhart," *Bear and Company* (June 1, 1985): 14.
18. John Reble, *The Church Hymnary*, rev. ed. (Oxford: Oxford University Press, 1927): 9.
19. Richard Wilbur, *Mayflies* (San Diego, New York, London: Harcourt Inc., 2000), 17.
20. David Daiches, *God and the Poets* (Oxford: Clarendon Press, 1984), 108.
21. W. H. Gardner, *Poems and Prose of Gerard Manley Hopkins* (Baltimore: Penguin Books, 1953), 51.
22. Ibid., 30.
23. Cited in *The Sense of the Sacramental*, ed. David Brown and Ann Loades (London: SPCK, 1995), 138.
24. Originally published in the journal *Weavings*; and also published in *Praxis*, the newsletter of Hartford Seminary, Hartford, CT; and in *Reflections* 90, no. 1 (Winter-Spring 1995): 19.
25. Originally published in *Presbyterian Outlook* (December 17, 2001): 12.
26. Ann Weems, "Peace, Peace . . . ," *Presbyterian Outlook*, August 16/23/30, 2004.
27. Originally published in *Christianity Today* (November 10, 1972): 6; and also published in *Presbyterian Outlook* 186, no. 26 (July 12, 2004): 12.
28. Saint John of the Cross, *The Flame of Love*, rev. ed., trans. Kieran Kavanaugh, OCD, and Otillo Rodriguez, OCD (Washington, DC: ICS Publications, 1991), stanza 4.

29. Frederick Buechner, *Brendan* (San Francisco: Harper & Row, 1988), 49f.

Chapter 2: An Imagining God

1. *Selected Plays of George Bernard Shaw,* vol. 2 (New York: Dodd, Mead & Co., 1949): 329.
2. Henry Ward Beecher, *The Yale Lectures on Preaching, First Series: Personal Elements in Preaching* (New York: J. B. Ford & Co., 1872), 109.
3. Ibid., 121.
4. Ibid.
5. John Baillie, *Our Knowledge of God* (London: Oxford University Press, 1939), 77.
6. The story runs that when the cardinal complained to the pope, his holiness refused to intervene on the grounds that his jurisdiction ceased at the gates of hell. The artist who was eventually hired to cover the offending genitalia, Daniele da Volterra, was forever after known as "the breeches painter."
7. Thomas H. Troeger, *Imagining a Sermon* (Nashville: Abingdon Press, 1990), 107.
8. Cheryl Forbes, *Imagination—Embracing a Theology of Wonder* (Portland, OR: Multnomah Press, 1986), 26.
9. Kenneth Patchen, *Hallelujah Anyway* (New York: New Directions Publishing Corp., 1967).
10. Eugene H. Peterson, *The Message: The Bible in Contemporary Language* (Colorado Springs, CO: NavPress, 2002), 1108.
11. Originally published in *Presbyterian Outlook* 185, no. 6 (February 17, 2003): 6.
12. William Muehl, *Why Preach? Why Listen?* (Philadelphia: Fortress Press, 1986), 46.
13. Ibid., 49.
14. Anne Carson, *Glass, Irony, and God* (New York: New Directions Publishing Corp., 1995), 49.
15. Muehl, *Why Peach? Why Listen?* 46.
16. Nicolai Berdyaev, *Christian Existentialism—A Berdyaev*

Synthesis Selected and Translated by Donald A. Lowrie (New York: Harper & Row, 1965), 152.

17. Ibid., 150.
18. C. S. Lewis, *Letters to Malcolm—Chiefly on Prayer* (San Diego, New York, London: Harcourt Brace & Co., 2002), 70.
19. I am indebted here to a discussion on pages 10–14 of *The Sense of the Sacramental—Movement and Measure in Art and Music, Place and Time*, ed. David Brown and Ann Loades (London: SPCK Press, 1995).
20. *The Paradiso of Dante Alighieri*, Temple Classics (London: J. M. Dent and Sons Ltd., 1930), 407.
21. Ibid., 409.
22. *Christian Century*, July 13–20, 1994.
23. Teilhard de Chardin, *The Divine Milieu* (New York: Harper & Row, 1960), 112.
24. Patrick Henry, *The Ironic Christian's Companion* (New York: Penguin Putnam, 1999), 74.
25. W. H. Gardner, *Poems and Prose of Gerard Manley Hopkins* (Baltimore: Penguin Books, 1953), 51.
26. Ibid., 27.
27. I no longer have my original notes from McIntyre's lecture, but he writes in very similar vein in his book *Faith, Theology, and Imagination* (Edinburgh: Handsell Press, 1987), 64.
28. *Selected Plays of George Bernard Shaw*, 329.
29. Warren Molton, *If God Is . . .* (Leavenworth, KS: Forest of Peace Publishing, 2002), 78.

Chapter 3: Steps toward Delight

1. Andre Malraux, *Anti–Memoirs* (New York: Holt, Rinehart & Winston, 1968), 2.
2. Dale Turner, *Different Seasons: Twelve Months of Wisdom and Inspiration* (Homewood, IL: High Tide Press, 1998).
3. Originally published in *Perspectives* 19, no. 2 (February 2004): 18.

4. Robert C. Dykstra, *Discovering a Sermon* (Saint Louis: Chalice Press, 2001), 75.
5. Brenda Ueland, *If You Want to Write—A Book about Art, Independence, and Spirit* (St. Paul: Graywolf Press, 1987), 32.
6. From the poem "Asphodel, That Greeny Flower," in William Carlos Williams, *Pictures from Brueghel and Other Poems* (New York: New Directions Books, 1962), 153–58.
7. Paul Griffiths, "Ringing in Words along with Fierce Spirit," *New York Times*, March 9, 2002, vol. 151, no. 52,052 p. B14.
8. Dykstra, *Discovering a Sermon*, 105.
9. Hugh MacDiarmid, *Selected Poems* (Harmondsworth, England: Penguin Books, 1970), 33.
10. Frederick Buechner, *The Final Beast* (New York: Seabury Press, 1965), 181–82.

Chapter 4: Looking for the Resurrection

1. *The Complete Works of William Shakespeare,* (New York: Oxford University Press, 1938), 919.
2. John W. Doberstein, *Minister's Prayer Book* (Philadelphia: Fortress Press, 1986).
3. Katherine S. White, *Onward and Upward in the Garden*, ed. by E. B. White (New York: Farrar, Straus & Giroux, 1979), xviii–xix.
4. *Christian Century*, April 19, 1991.
5. Originally published in *Reflections* 90, no. 1 (Winter-Spring 1995): 20.
6. Robert Frost, *The Poetry of Robert Frost*, ed. Edward Connery Latham (New York: Holt, Rinehart, & Winston, 1969), 177.
7. Originally published in *A.D.* 2, no. 9 (September 1973): 56.
8. *Christian Century*, June 29, 2004.
9. J. Barrie Shepherd, *Seeing with the Soul: Daily Meditations on the Parables of Jesus in Luke* (1991; repr., Louisville, KY: Westminster John Knox Press, 2004).

10. Troeger, *Imagining a Sermon*, 97.
11. Richard Wilbur, *New and Collected Poems* (San Diego, New York, London: Harcourt Brace Jovanovich, 1989), 233f.
12. Wallace Stevens, *The Necessary Angel* (New York: Random House, 1965), 29f.
13. Loretta Ross-Gotta, *Letters from the Holy Ground* (Franklin, WI: Sheed & Ward, 2000), 44.
14. Julian Hartt, *Theological Method and Imagination* (New York: Seabury Press, 1977), 107.
15. *Christian Century*, January 24, 1996.
16. Brueggemann, *Finally Comes the Poet* (Minneapolis: Fortress Press, 1989), 73f.
17. James S. Stewart, *The Gates of New Life* (London: Hodder & Staughton, 1973), 186.

Chapter 5: Delight in Action

1. The Battell Chapel of Yale University was the setting for this sermon, on Sunday, October 13, 2002. The Yale Divinity School convocation, at which I was to deliver the Lyman Beecher Lectures, opened later that day, and the tradition was that the Beecher lecturer preached at university worship on that morning. Scripture readings were Isaiah 40:13–17, Psalm 46, Luke 9:18–25, and 1 Corinthians 1:25–28.
2. Henri J. M. Nouwen, *The Way of the Heart* (New York: Ballantine Books, 1991), 33.
3. *Oeuvres de sully prudhomme: poésies, 1865–1866, stances et poèmes* (Paris: Alphonse Lemerre), 188, 23–33 passage choisel.
4. Thomas Merton, *Raids on the Unspeakable* (New York: New Directions, 1966), 17.
5. *The Complete Poems of Emily Dickinson*, ed. Thomas H. Johnson, (Boston: Back Bay Books, Little, Brown & Co., 1961), 710.
6. David F. K. Steindl-Rast, *Multi-Media Worship*, ed. Myron R. Bloy Jr. (New York: Seabury Press, 1969), 65.

7. This sermon was preached on Sunday, February 22, 2004, at Bradley Hills Presbyterian Church, in suburban Washington, DC. Bradley Hills was the home congregation of then General Assembly moderator Susan Andrews. The Old Testament lesson for the service was Psalm 1. The New Testament lesson was Romans 14:4–13.

8. John Baillie, *And the Life Everlasting* (New York: Charles Scribner's Sons, 1933), 289.

9. In the summer of 2004, at the 217th General Assembly of the Presbyterian Church (U.S.A.) held in Richmond, VA, I was privileged to be one of the preachers at assembly worship. The following sermon was preached on Thursday, July 1, in the Greater Richmond Convention Center. The Old Testament reading was Psalm 148, the New Testament, John 9:1–12.

10. Alfred Lord Tennyson, *The Higher Pantheism* (1847), vi.

Acknowledgments

"Love Calls Us to the Things of This World" from *Things of This World*, copyright © 1956 and renewed 1984 by Richard Wilbur. Reprinted by permission of Harcourt, Inc. and from *New and Collected Poems* by Richard Wilbur, © 1988 by Richard Wilbur. Reprinted by permission of Faber and Faber Ltd.

"Mayflies" from *Mayflies: New Poems and Translations*, copyright © 2000 by Richard Wilbur, reprinted by permission of Harcourt, Inc.

"Peace, Peace . . . " from *The Presbyterian Outlook*, August 16/23/30, 2004, copyright 2004 by Ann Weems.

Excerpt from "Peaches, page 27," from *American Sonnets* by Gerald Stern, copyright © 2002 by Gerald Stern. Used by permission of W. W. Norton & Company, Inc.

"Two Porpoises Passed By" by Barrie Shepherd, copyright 1993 *Christian Century*. Reprinted by permission from the April 14, 1993, issue of the *Christian Century*.

"Cosmicology" by Barrie Shepherd, copyright 1994 *Christian Century*. Reprinted by permission from the July 13–20, 1994, issue of the *Christian Century*.

"Un-dividing Wall" by Barrie Shepherd, copyright 1991 *Christian Century*. Reprinted by permission from the April 19, 1991, issue of the *Christian Century*.

"Clock Minder" by Barrie Shepherd, copyright 1996 *Christian Century*. Reprinted by permission from the January 24, 1996, issue of the *Christian Century*.

"Hummers" by Barrie Shepherd, copyright 2004 *Christian Century*. Reprinted by permission from the June 29, 2004, issue of the *Christian Century*.

CPSIA information can be obtained at www.ICGtesting.com
Printed in the USA
LVOW11s0821031015

456808LV00001B/131/P